TEDDY & JOSIE

TEDDY & JOSIE

BOOK ONE
THE ADVENTURE BEGINS

Master Rose Ashley

gatekeeper press™

Columbus, Ohio

Teddy & Josie

Published by Gatekeeper Press
2167 Stringtown Rd, Suite 109
Columbus, OH 43123-2989
www.GatekeeperPress.com

Library of Congress Control Number: 2021940967

ISBN (hardcover): 9781662915925
ISBN (paperback): 9781662915932
eISBN: 9781662915949

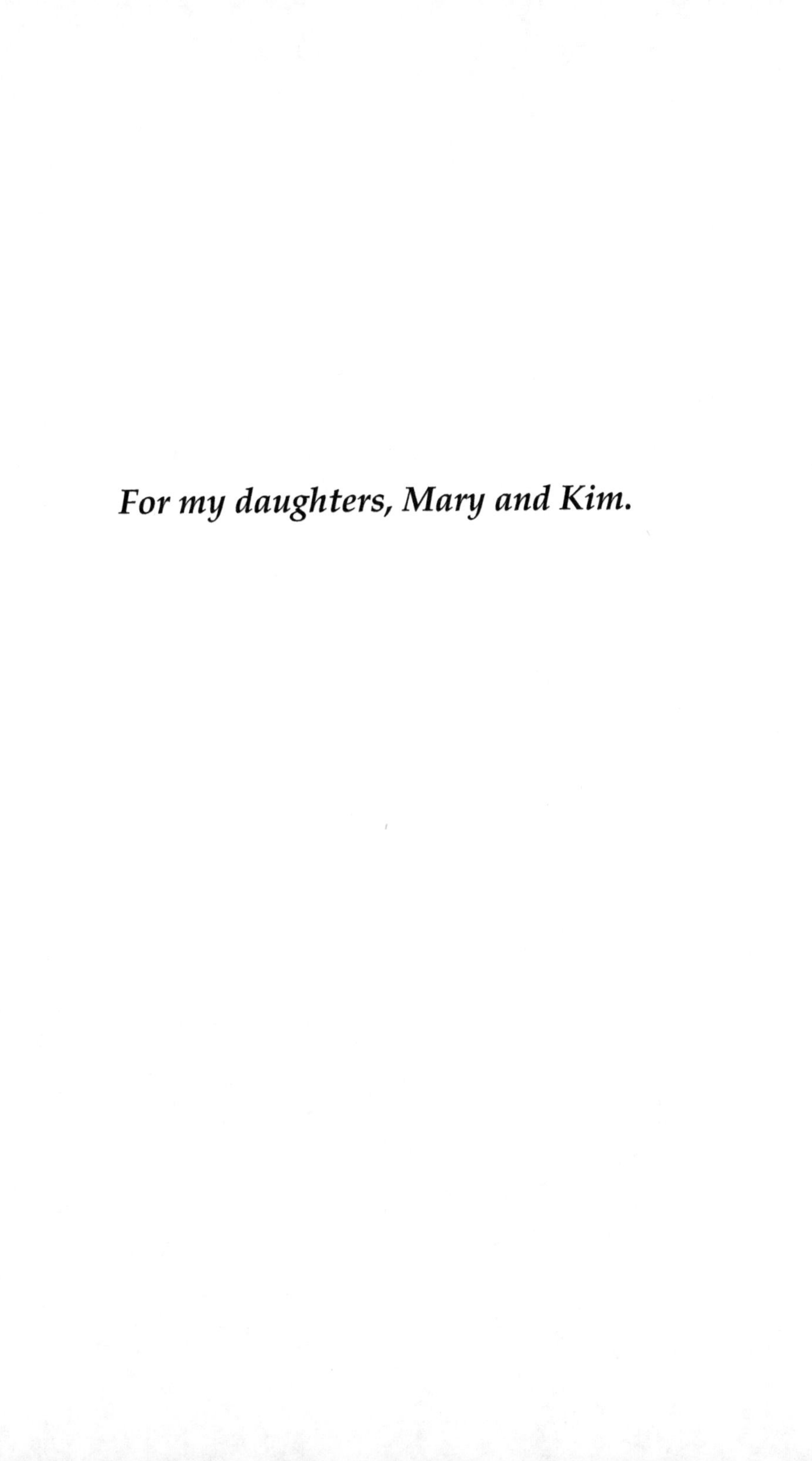

For my daughters, Mary and Kim.

Acknowledgment

I would like to sincerely acknowledge and thank my long-time friend, spiritual student, and business partner, Fran Hughes. Her dedication, love, and support assisted me greatly in my revision of the original *Teddy & Josie Book One* to the present-day edition. She spent countless hours attending to the administrative and production details with the publisher, reviewing the written work, and serving as an unbiased sounding board and motivator. Her words of encouragement were priceless. She has the patience of a saint and is a whiz kid extraordinaire!

Many thanks to Rob Price, CEO of Gatekeeper Press, Nicole, the author manager assigned to *Teddy & Josie Book One*, and Gatekeeper's production staff. They gave true meaning to Gatekeeper's motto, "Where authors are family." Rob's integrity, professionalism, and commitment to the author were ever-present. Nicole was the light in the dark, patiently guiding us through the publishing process. She was kind, professional, easy to reach, and quick to respond to our seemingly endless questions and changes. I am truly looking forward to the next journey with Gatekeeper Press for the publication of *Teddy & Josie Book Two*.

CHAPTER 1

A WISH FULFILLED

A small blue figure sailed through Josie's window, riding high on a wisp of cool night air. It followed the breeze across the room and then, with arms outstretched and back erect, slowly drifted down onto a pillow next to the sleeping boy.

Early the next morning, sunlight filtered into the cheery bedroom, first in thin bands, then bursting full and wide. Josie winced, then blinked as he rubbed the sleepiness from his eyes. He opened one eye and then quickly the other. When Josie spied the blue figure, he jumped out of bed, heart pounding, and grabbed a slipper to defend himself. Then, as he began his best swat, he heard the creature call out. "No, stop!" Josie froze on the spot. The last thing he expected was for it to talk.

"What are you?" Josie screamed out.

"Good heavens," the little blue creature exclaimed. "You needn't holler. My ears may be small, but they function quite well, thank you. And it's not what are you, but who are you?"

"All right then. Who are you?" Josie continued.

"My name is Theodore Bearingsworth the Third, but you may call me Teddy unless you are introducing me to royalty, of course."

Josie rubbed his eyes even harder than before, but Teddy was still there when he stopped and opened them. A cloud of shimmering, blue dust billowed around Teddy then settled onto the bed, forming a small pile.

"Gosh, you're not blue, after all," Josie exclaimed.

"No, no, I'm just covered in blue dust. Can't say that I mind, though considering," Teddy said while patting his neatly pressed white shirt and sky-blue bow tie, jacket, and trousers.

"Where did you come from?" Josie asked, still not believing what he was seeing.

"And how did you get here?"

"I came here from another realm in answer to your wish. Last night as you were dozing off, you were reflecting on how lost and confused you felt. You sincerely wished that someone would help you. Well, here I am, at your service." Josie stared in disbelief.

"And this is my hello gift," Teddy continued while pointing to the blue dust.

Teddy put his hand into his trousers' pocket and withdrew a small, red velvet pouch attached to a slender gold chain. He quickly scooped the dust into the pouch. With each new addition, the bag grew in size to accommodate its contents. Finally, when the bag was filled to the brim, Teddy instructed Josie to bend down so that he could fasten the chain around his neck.

"There. Wear it always. Whenever you have a problem, just sprinkle some of this dust around you, and everything will be A-OK."

Josie was so distracted by Teddy's arrival that he completely forgot it was a school day. His mother called out, "Breakfast," and this spurred Josie into high gear. In a matter of minutes, he had dressed, brushed his teeth, and combed his hair. It was a relief to have something familiar to think about and do. He grabbed his backpack and bounded across the room towards the door.

"Hey!" Teddy shouted. "What about me? I'm hungry too!"

"Well, what should I do with you?" Josie asked.

"I could ride on your shoulder," Teddy suggested. "That way, I wouldn't have to strain my voice to be heard."

"What if my mother sees you?"

"I wouldn't worry about that," Teddy responded.

Josie didn't have time to question what Teddy meant because his mother was already calling him for a second time. So, he gently lifted Teddy onto his shoulder. Teddy wiggled in place, tugged at the bottom of his vest, and straightened his bow tie before grabbing onto Josie's ear lobe.

Josie reluctantly entered the kitchen, walking a little sideways, hoping to camouflage Teddy.

"Don't worry," Teddy whispered.

"She won't be aware of my presence. I'm like a crack in the wall to her."

"A crack in the wall?" Josie questioned.

"Yes, when there is a crack in the wall, you may notice it at first, but over time, if you don't focus on it, you will reach a point where you aren't aware of it at all."

"So, she could see you if she wanted to?" Josie asked as he sat down at the table.

"Most definitely," Teddy answered. "She just needs to expand her awareness."

Teddy could tell, by the puzzled look on Josie's face, that he needed more information. "Awareness is like a zoomable flashlight, which allows you to twist the head to adjust the width of the light. You can easily light up an entire room, or you can narrow the light down to zoom in on just one object. Awareness operates the same way. We can expand our awareness to experience all of creation or decrease it and only experience a small portion. Your mother is only aware of what exists in the physical reality."

"So, you don't exist in the physical reality? You're not real?" Josie asked as he furrowed his brow.

Teddy let out a hearty laugh. "Things don't have to be physical to be real, laddie."

Mrs. Alester placed a waffle and maple syrup on the table. Teddy perked up and asked, "Is that real maple syrup?" Josie responded with a nod to the affirmative. Sadly, Josie didn't have much of an appetite. He didn't want food. He wanted answers.

"Are you a fairy, Teddy?"

"Yes, lad, I am. Brilliant deduction."

"I wasn't sure since you're not all dressed in green."

"Green," Teddy responded with an air of indignation. "You're not confusing me with a Leprechaun, I hope."

"What's the difference?" asked Josie.

"The difference? Why there's all the difference in the world. Fairies are fairies, and leprechauns are, well, leprechauns."

"Quit murmuring, Josie." Mrs. Alester interrupted. "Eat your food before it gets cold."

Josie quickly ate his waffle, nervous the whole time that his mother's awareness might suddenly return. If it did, he would have a lot more to explain than why he kept putting little pieces of waffle up to his shoulder (smothered, much to Teddy's delight, in real maple syrup).

Josie finished his breakfast, gathered his things, said goodbye to his mother, and ran out the door.

"Hang on, Teddy. I'll have to run to catch the school bus."

Teddy used both hands to clutch onto Josie's ear and prepared himself for the ride. Bump, bump, thump, thump. He bounced up and down and nearly lost his grip.

Josie arrived at the bus stop just as the bus pulled up. He hurried up the steps and looked for a seat. His spirits dropped when he realized that the only spot left was behind Butch Kellogg, the class bully. Josie reluctantly sat down, turned to Teddy, and asked if the ride on his shoulder had been too rough.

"No, no, it was just like life - a great adventure."

Josie continued talking to Teddy in hushed tones. A few minutes later, Butch whipped around with a sneer on his face. "Hey, dummy, talking to yourself?"

"No, I'm not." Josie shot back defensively. "I'm talking to my new friend, Teddy. He's a fairy."

"Wow, you're even dumber than I thought," Butch said with a snicker. "I bet you still believe in Santa Claus too."

Josie felt angry with himself for telling Butch that he had a fairy friend. Teddy tugged on Josie's ear and pointed to the red velvet bag.

"Sprinkle some around."

Josie quickly reached into the bag, extracted a small amount of the special dust, and let it fall. It swirled around for a moment and then disappeared. As if by magic, his anger left, and he became filled with a tremendous sense of joy. Butch swung around like a shot and began to giggle. He smiled at Josie and seemed very happy.

"Wow!" Josie exclaimed. "What is this stuff?"

"It's a reminder of true happiness," Teddy said with a twinkle in his eyes.

"Happiness?" Josie questioned.

"No, not just plain, old, run-of-the-mill happiness," Teddy stated. "True Happiness."

"What's the difference?" Josie asked.

"Well, when people are content or having fun and laughing, they might think they are truly happy, but true happiness is so much more than that. It bubbles up from deep inside of you and spills out all over everything outside of you. It's very energizing and uplifting, inspires kindness, and motivates you to do great things."

"Well, whatever you call it, it works," Josie said. "Butch always picks on me. He's the meanest kid in the whole school."

"I don't think he's mean, Josie. He's just lonely, afraid, and hurting, so he takes those feelings out on others."

"You're awfully smart, Teddy. Do you know everything?"

"Oh, my," Teddy chuckled with a glint in his eyes. "Let's just say I have access to a great deal of knowledge."

Josie didn't spend much time reflecting on Teddy's answer before blurting out, "I'm so upset that Butch thinks I still believe in Santa Claus. I'm not a baby. I know Santa isn't real."

"Ahem," Teddy started. "I happen to be good friends with the man, and he would not like to hear that he isn't real."

Josie was stunned. "You know Santa Claus?"

"Yes, indeed. Santa Claus, the Easter Bunny, the Tooth Fairy, and Cupid are all good friends of mine and lots of fun at a party if you can imagine. They all exist in another realm. Would you like to visit them?"

"Oh, can I?" asked Josie.

"Of course, you can. I'll arrange it for this very evening."

The rest of the day dragged by for Josie, and then to make matters worse, his teacher, Mrs. Cragg, announced a surprise test in math.

"Oh, no!" Josie exclaimed with a frown on his face. "My worst subject."

"Have no fear," Teddy said. "Use the special dust."

Josie perked up and reached into the small bag. He withdrew a pinch of the dust, sprinkled it around, and immediately felt more confident. One math answer after another popped into his head, and soon, in no time at all, he had finished the test. Josie was amazed and surprised, but Teddy wasn't. He knew that all of our problems are easily solved when we are truly happy.

The final bell of the day rang out at the end of Josie's math class. He quickly put his books into his backpack and headed for the door. He was anxious to meet up with his friend Maryann Models. Maryann liked to be called Mary for short, and she preferred to spell her name with an "i" instead of a "y." Mary and Josie had been neighbors ever since they were babies, and Josie couldn't remember a time when Mary wasn't his friend.

Mary didn't attend the same school as Josie, but every day after classes, they would meet at the local park to share the events of their day. Mary was accompanied that day, as usual, by her spunky, black poodle named Bonji. Bonji was an exceptional dog, as evidenced by her proud gait. She carried her head, ever just so, to display the new rhinestone collar awarded her for taking first place in the city dog show. Bonji jumped up and wagged her tail when she saw Josie approaching but then began to bark and bark and bark.

"Bonji!" Mary called out. "Why are you making so much noise? You know, Josie."

"She's barking at me," Teddy whispered to Josie.

"You mean Bonji can see you?" Josie asked.

"Certainly," Teddy answered while tipping his blue derby hat to Bonji.

"Animals are very, very aware. Why I've had some of my most enlightening conversations about the sacred Hu, with an anteater named Dasral."

"The sacred who?" Josie asked.

"Not who," Teddy responded. "Hu – capital H, little u. It is an ancient word for God."

"Hi Josie," Mary called out, in that wonderfully warm and loving way that she always did.

Josie could hardly contain his excitement as he responded. "Hey, Mary, do you notice anything different about me today?"

"Yeah, you're late."

"No, I mean, do you see anything unusual, like maybe around my left shoulder."

"Nope, should I?"

"I was hoping you would," Josie answered with disappointment in his voice.

"Mary?"

"Yes."

"Do you believe in fairies?"

"Fairies, like the Tooth Fairy or a Fairy Godmother?"

Josie nodded his head.

"No. That's little kid stuff."

Josie's heart sank when he realized he couldn't even share Teddy with his best friend.

"Don't worry," Teddy whispered. "Just keep loving and appreciating Mary for who she is and for who she has been for you. Friends don't have to experience the same reality to share a life together."

Josie was happy to hear this. The news lifted his spirit and caused him to think deeply about the many things he loved about Mary. She was fun and funny, and her laugh was like no other. You could be feeling down or sad or upset, and her laugh would always transport you to a happier place. Mary was kind, caring, and loyal. Josie felt as if he had known her forever. He often had dreams of them together in other lands and other bodies. He liked these dreams but wasn't quite sure why he had them.

Time seemed to speed by whenever Josie was with Mary, and that day was no exception. They said their goodbyes, and Josie headed for home. When he opened the front door, he was greeted by a house full of tempting aromas. He heard his mother humming in the kitchen as she baked cookies.

"What a great day," Josie said to Teddy. "You came into my life and gave me the special dust. I aced my math test, and now, cookies!" Josie felt so exuberant that he decided to share the events of his day with his mother. "Mom, I met a new friend today."

"That's wonderful," she said while smiling.

"His name is Teddy, and he's a fairy."

Mrs. Alester's smile slid right off of her face. "Now, Josie, don't you think your imagination is running a bit wild?"

"No, Mom, he's here right now, on my left shoulder."

Mrs. Alester approached Josie and peered very closely at his shoulder.

"Josie, there isn't anything there. Now no more talk of this nonsense."

Mrs. Alester walked over to the oven to remove a batch of cookies, shaking her head as she did. Josie glanced over at his fairy friend and began to doubt his presence. Teddy immediately started to fade away, so he yelled, "Hey!" right into Josie's ear. Josie's ear smarted, and he could not deny that Teddy was definitely there.

"You started to fade away," Josie said.

"I didn't go anywhere," Teddy explained. "Your awareness of me decreased because of your doubt. If you want to experience things beyond the *Physical*, you will need to believe that all things are possible."

That evening the Alester's dinner was served promptly at 6:00, as always. Teddy became very excited when he saw the tossed salad and parmesan cheese dressing. He loved good food almost as much as good company.

Josie's parents were in a cheerful mood. They began chatting about the events of their day as Mrs. Alester passed the mashed potatoes around the table. Josie noticed that Teddy was sitting quietly, with his eyes closed and head bowed.

"What's wrong?" Josie whispered.

Teddy opened his eyes and reassured Josie that nothing was wrong.

"I always bow my head and say a blessing to express my gratitude before I eat a meal. I also say it when I wake up in the morning and at the end of my day because you can never be too grateful. I close my eyes, focus on the love I feel for all of God's creations, and then say the blessing."

Thank you, God, for all that I am
And for all that I can be.

Thank you for all that I love
And for all who love me.

Thank you for the many blessings
I have received, and I pray
that I will always be a blessing
in return to thee.

Josie's parents paused their conversation and turned towards Josie. Mr. Alester spoke up. "Well, son, how was your day?"

"It was okay, Dad, but I need to talk to you about something important."

"Sure, son, what is it?" He asked while passing the salad.

"Do you see something unusual on my left shoulder?" Josie continued while pointing to Teddy.

Mr. Alester got up to inspect for a possible problem, and as he reached for Josie's shoulder, he knocked Teddy off. Teddy landed abruptly right into the bowl of mashed potatoes. Josie leaped to his feet and screamed. "Teddy, Teddy, where are you?"

Teddy gasped. "Here! Hurry! In the potatoes, I'm sinking fast. Helllp!"

Josie dove for the potatoes and began digging through them with his hands. He spotted Teddy and pulled him out by the arms. It was only then that he noticed the horrified looks on his parent's faces. Their shock quickly turned into displeasure, and Mr. Alester was the first one to speak.

"Just what was the meaning of that display?" he said, his voice rising.

"I'm sorry, Dad, but you knocked Teddy into the mashed potatoes. He was suffocating."

"Teddy? Who in the world is Teddy?"

"He's, he's a, a fairy," Josie stammered.

"Oh, no," Mrs. Alester added. "You're still not on that fairy nonsense, are you?"

"It's not nonsense," cried Josie. "Teddy is real," Josie explained while reaching inside his shirt and pulling out the little red bag.

"Teddy gave me this bag full of special dust."

Josie's mother opened the bag and looked inside. "Just as I thought. It's empty."

Mr. Alester's neck was beginning to turn red, a sure sign of imminent trouble.

"Go to your room," he said in a very restrained voice.

Josie slowly rose from his chair and picked up Teddy, who was just then recovering from his narrow escape. They made a sorry-looking pair as they left the room - one dejected little boy and one very goopy fairy.

Teddy and Josie both agreed that a bath was in order. So, Josie filled his tub with warm water and bubbles and prepared the bathroom basin in the same manner for Teddy. Then, Josie entered his bath and began reflecting on the events of the day. He stayed in the tub, lost in thought, until the bubbles were all gone, and the water was no longer appealing. When he got out, he dried off, dressed in his pajamas, and fashioned a lovely little bed for Teddy. When he finished, he called out to Teddy, "Are you almost done?"

"Ah, yes," Teddy answered. "I just got the last of the potatoes out of my ears."

Teddy dried off with a fluffy hand towel, wrapped it around himself, and appeared next to Josie. "I wanted to make a nightshirt for you," Josie said. "I found some scraps of material in my Mom's sewing room, but I've never sewn anything before."

"Ah, but you have," Teddy said. "In another time and another place."

"What other time and place?" asked Josie.

"Well, this may come as a surprise to you, lad, but you have lived many other lives in many other places."

"I have?" Josie said in amazement. "Why don't I remember them?"

"Well, some memories are more difficult to recall than others due to the mechanics of the mind. The mind, you see, has three storage areas referred to as the conscious mind, the subconscious mind, and the unconscious mind. The best analogy that I can think of is a computer. A computer has a viewing screen, files, folders, and a hard drive.

Our conscious mind is like an open file displayed on a computer screen. Our subconscious mind is like a computer folder that contains multiple files. If we want to read a file, we can easily open the folder, select a file and display it on the screen."

"I see," Josie responded. "Like my math test today. My conscious mind held some of the answers, and the special dust helped me to reach into my subconscious to find the rest."

"Yes, Laddie. Very good." Teddy smiled and then continued his tutorial.

"The unconscious mind is like a computer hard drive where permanent computer data is stored. We can retrieve information from a computer hard drive, but for the most part, we are not even aware that it exists. The same holds true of the unconscious mind."

"Can you give me an example of this?" Josie asked.

"Yes," Teddy continued. "At some point in time, you learned how to add one plus one. It's easy for you to recall this knowledge because it is stored in your subconscious. It is not, however, as easy to recall what you wore to school or what the weather was like on the day that you learned how to add because the mind stored those memories in the unconscious."

"Is that where my past life memories are stored?" Josie asked.

"Yes, laddie."

"How can I call up memories from my unconscious mind?"

"As your awareness increases, you will naturally become more aware of what is stored in the unconscious. But, for now, we will depend on a little help from the special dust so you can remember how to sew."

Teddy helped himself to some of the blue dust and sprinkled it over Josie's head. Josie threaded a needle. Initially, it felt awkward in his fingers, but then it seemed to take on a life of its own and began guiding Josie's work with the fabric. "This is neat," Josie stated to no one in particular. "I'm sewing!" A short time later, Teddy modeled the finished product – a flannel nightshirt worthy of envy.

"Perfect," he hummed. "Perfect!"

"I have a surprise for you, Teddy," Josie said humbly.

"You do?"

"Yes, close your eyes."

Teddy complied. Josie lifted him to the top of his bureau and set him down inside an old cigar box, which Josie had lined with cotton batting covered with swatches of mint green satin.

"Like it, Teddy? I made it when you were taking your bath."

Teddy opened his eyes. They gleamed and sparkled as only fairy eyes can.

"For me?" he asked bashfully.

"Yes, Teddy, your very own bed."

Josie rolled up a scrap of rose-colored velvet and handed it to Teddy, "Your pillow, Mr. Bearingsworth."

Teddy placed the soft pillow down and slipped between the pieces of satin.

"Fit for a king," he sighed.

Josie propped his elbows on the bureau, rested his head on his hands, and sighed.

"Teddy?"

"Yes, lad."

"I have so many questions," Josie sighed.

Teddy sat up, yawned, and said, "Well, ask away."

"This morning, you said that you came from another realm. What's a realm?"

"Realms are states of consciousness that you can visit and experience."

"So, states of consciousness are individual realms?"

"Yes, they are like the states in the United States of America. They each exist as a separate realm, but when you put them all together, they form one large realm."

Josie was fascinated. "How many realms are there?"

"There are five lower realms and a multitude of higher realms. The lowest realm is the *Physical* – the one you are the most familiar with. The next realm is the *Astral* – the realm of dreams and emotions. The third is the *Causal* – the realm of the past, present, and future. The fourth is the *Mental* – the realm of the mind. The fifth is the *Intuitive* – the realm of sensing and feeling. This realm connects you to your real self - a spiritual being composed of light and sound. You may think of yourself as just the walking, talking boy known as Josie Alester, but the real you is so much more than that, as you will soon discover. I will teach you about the higher realms at a later time, as they are not easy to describe with words. They are better understood when experienced."

Josie took a deep breath to let the information sink in, and then he continued, "What does consciousness mean?"

"Consciousness means awareness. It refers to those things that you are presently aware of – the things you are presently experiencing. For example, when you are awake, you are aware of the *Physical*. When you sleep and dream, you lose your physical awareness and become aware of the *Astral*. When you wake up and return to the *Physical*, the *Astral* is still there, but you are no longer aware of it."

"I also don't understand why Mom didn't see the blue dust when she looked into the bag," Josie continued.

Teddy stroked his chin and answered, "The things we see in life are often colored by our previous experiences. It's like looking through a pair of blue-lensed sunglasses. Everything you see appears to be blue. You receive a distorted view of things. When your mother looked into the velvet bag, she was looking through the lenses of a life devoid of true happiness."

"Will she ever be able to see it?"

"Yes, laddie, as your mother's awareness increases, so will her ability to experience true happiness. Josie felt comforted hearing this and paused for a moment of reflection before asking, "And how do anteaters talk?"

Teddy chuckled. "You mean, my friend, Dasral? Well, animals, insects, and plants all have a special way of communicating."

"Plants!" exclaimed Josie.

"Yes," Teddy continued, "Even plants. All of God's creations can communicate with each other and with people. They do it all the time. The problem is that people aren't always aware enough to notice."

"Can you teach me to talk to all of the creations, Teddy?"

"Yes, of course, but not just now. We should sleep before we embark on our journey."

"I'm kind of worried about that," Josie shared. "I don't think I can just leave in the middle of the night to go on a journey. What if my parents come into my room to check on me, and they see that I'm not here?"

"If your parents come in, they will see your body, in your bed, sleeping soundly, but you will be someplace else."

"I don't understand. How can I go anywhere without my body?"

"You don't need your physical body to travel to other realms. You can use your other bodies."

"I have more than one body?"

"Yes, lad. When you were born, you were given the use of five bodies, one for each of the lower realms. You have a physical body, an astral body, a causal body, a mental body, and an intuitive body. They wrap around you like gloves over a hand."

"I think I understand," Josie said. "The real me is a spiritual being composed of light and sound who uses five bodies, one physical and four non-physical, to experience the lower realms."

"Yes, laddie, you get an A+!"

Teddy yawned and said, "Now we should sleep and rest up for the night's journey."

CHAPTER 2

THE JOURNEY BEGINS

The old grandfather clock in the entrance hall struck midnight. Teddy tweaked Josie's nose and told him to wake up.

"But, Teddy," he protested. "It's the middle of the night."

"Yes, yes," was Teddy's quick reply. "The best time to travel to the other realms. Hurry up, or we'll miss the train."

"What train?"

"The *Dream Train*. It will be coming by momentarily."

Josie was on his feet in no time and looked out the window. "I don't see it," he said grumpily.

"That's because your eyes are open," answered Teddy. "Now come here, or we'll miss it."

A very bewildered Josie sat down on his bed next to Teddy.

"Close your eyes," Teddy began. "Take a few deep, relaxing breaths, and focus on your third eye."

"My third eye," Josie exclaimed. "I don't have three eyes."

"Yes, you do," Teddy continued. "You have two physical eyes and one non-physical spiritual eye. Your physical eyes allow you to see the physical realm. Your spiritual eye, which is called the third eye, enables you to see the other realms. If you close your physical eyes, take a few relaxing breaths and concentrate on the area in the middle of your forehead, your spiritual eye will open. You can also sing the sacred Hu word to speed up the process."

Josie closed his physical eyes, took a few relaxing breaths, and joined Teddy in a Hu song. They began singing in unison – singing, stopping simultaneously to take a breath, then singing again. Josie could hear both his voice and Teddy's as two separate sounds. Then at some point, their voices merged and formed a single sound. It reminded Josie of bees buzzing independently of each other yet creating one unified sound.

Josie felt like he was floating. He opened his eyes and saw that he was. He had risen upwards, and when he looked down, he saw himself asleep in his bed.

"What's happening?" Josie asked Teddy, who was hovering next to him. "How am I up here and down there at the same time?"

"You're not," Teddy explained. "Your real self is up here, while your physical body is down there. Don't worry. You won't need it where we are going. You will be using your other bodies."

"But what if I leave my physical body, and I can't find it again?"

"You won't lose it," Teddy reassured Josie. "You are connected to it by a cord of energy. If you look closely, you will see it."

Josie looked down at his physical body. Sure enough, he saw a thin, silver cord of energy connecting his physical body to his floating self. It reminded him of pictures he had seen of astronauts on a spacewalk, tethered to their spaceship by a long cord. After that, Josie felt more at ease, knowing that he wouldn't lose his physical body.

"OK, Teddy, I understand."

"Good. Now let's get back to our journey."

The two travelers closed their eyes and continued singing the Hu song. Within minutes, Josie's third eye opened, and he saw a train. It was not your ordinary everyday sort of train. It was sky-blue and shimmering as if it had been painted with the special dust. A brilliant white light radiated from the engine's front, and a smokestack spewed out thousands of particles of stardust. It was a magnificent-looking vehicle. The engine was followed by so many cars that Josie could not see the end. Each car was filled to the brim with people, critters of all types, and toys. There was even a very tall car reserved for giraffes so they could stretch their long necks and a very wide one for lady elephants. They wear such big hats, you know.

As the train drew closer, Josie could hear the noise of the engine. Instead of going chug a lug, chug a lug, it talked, and what it said was, "All you have to do is Hu, all you have to do is Hu."

"All aboard," called the station master. "All aboard for the *Astral*."

Teddy and Josie moved along with a group of antelope and caterpillars and boarded the second car from the engine. They chose seats towards the back, so they could take in all of the activity.

"Tickets, please, tickets," shouted a lady kangaroo wearing a red cap with the word *Conductor* on it. She walked down the aisle, collecting tickets and stuffing each one into her generous pouch.

Josie turned to Teddy with a concerned look on his face.

"I don't have a ticket."

"Sure you do," quipped Teddy. "The Hu is your ticket."

Before long, they were on their way. Josie hung his head out of the window to watch the big train's wheels turn. It was then that he noticed the train did not travel on tracks. Instead, it drifted along above the ground on a cushion of light, which emitted all sorts of mystical sounds.

"What is that?" Josie asked Teddy while pointing out the window.

"It's the *Sound Current*. It guides the train and us to all of the various realms. Each realm emanates a unique sound. So, if you follow its sound, it will lead you there."

"How do I pick just one?" Josie asked. "It seems like a lot of different sounds are all playing at the same time."

"Listening to the *Sound Current* is similar to listening to an orchestra. You can focus your attention on the unified sound of the instruments playing in harmony, or you can focus on a single sound. For example, if you concentrate on the violins, you can hear them in the forefront and the other instruments in the background. It is the same with the *Sound Current*. You can focus on the unified sound or on a single sound. It can seem challenging when you first attempt to do this, but it will become easier with practice."

As the train glided along, Josie became aware of conversations taking place amongst the other passengers. He understood everything they were communicating, even though no words were spoken aloud. In place of words, Josie heard thoughts and felt feelings. He was deeply engrossed in observing the process when a friendly yellow duck waddled up. Without saying a word, he conveyed to Josie and Teddy that his name was Mr. Waddles. Much to Josie's delight, he was able to respond in thought. A silent exchange of information continued for the rest of the ride. Mr. Waddles told Josie of wondrous places he had visited and about someone he referred to as the *Inner Master*. Teddy shared that he had met the *Inner Master* as well. A sleek black cat named Midnight joined the conversation and said that she knew this same being as the *Grand Teacher*. Josie noticed that even though they disagreed on a name, they were in complete agreement that this individual was, above all, very kind, loving, and knowledgeable. Josie expressed a desire to meet the *Inner Master*, and they all responded in unison, "When the student is ready, the Master will appear."

Josie was becoming a little nervous about what he might encounter when they got to the *Astral*, so he shared this with Teddy.

"The *Astral* will surprise you in many ways," Teddy began. "One of my favorites is that it is not limited by time. We can travel there in our dream bodies for just a few minutes and experience an adventure that would have taken hours, days, or weeks to transpire in the *Physical*. You will also notice that the *Astral* closely resembles the *Physical*. It is similar to a movie studio with all the props and scenery we would ever want or need to create a film of our choice. Only in this instance, it's not a movie we are making; it's a life. We visit the *Astral*, choose the things we want to experience, then serve as channels for them to travel through and manifest in the *Physical*. For example, a songwriter visits the *Astral*, hears a song, feels inspired by it, then serves as a channel for it to come through to the *Physical*. The same holds true of artists, book writers, architects, inventors, and so on. We can also channel life scenarios, both positive and negative."

"I don't remember choosing the scenarios I have in my life," Josie stated.

"Well, unfortunately, our subconscious and unconscious thoughts and beliefs greatly influence what we channel, so we aren't always consciously aware of our choices. That is why it is important to expand your awareness, so you aren't caught off guard by what you are manifesting."

Josie sat in silence and vowed to focus on expanding his awareness so he wouldn't accidentally manifest any bad stuff.

A short time later, the train came to a halt, and the conductor announced their arrival at the *Astral*. The moment Josie stepped out of the train, he was filled with joy. Colored lights flashed all around him, and rainbows filled the powder blue skies. Birds flew in abundance, and flowers of every type and hue looked up at them. Soul-stirring music filled the air, and butterflies drifted on the notes.

"Teddy, I think I just saw an angel," Josie said.

"It's possible," Teddy answered. "On the *Astral*, all things are possible. Come now, we have an appointment with Santa Claus and the Easter Bunny. They are at the *Dream Palace*."

"How do we get there?" Josie asked.

"We are there," Teddy responded. "See!" The scenery shifted immediately, and they were looking across a wide, deep moat, which surrounded a golden castle. Josie was about to ask how they would cross the moat when a striking white horse with magnificent wings appeared before them. He knelt, bowed his head, and extended one of his wings, inviting Josie and Teddy to climb onto his back. As soon as they were mounted, their steed took one mighty leap and began to fly. Josie felt so incredibly free as a surge of energy passed through his body. But quicker than you could say, "Hu," the stallion descended in front of a spectacular castle door. He whinnied three times, and the door swung open. Josie jumped down, entered the castle, and there, before his very eyes, resting on a red velvet hammock, was Santa Claus. Josie was thrilled. Santa looked up and motioned with his finger for Josie to come closer.

"Ho, Ho, Ho, and hello, Josie, we've been waiting for you," he said, nodding towards the Easter Bunny, who was finger-painting ostrich eggs. The stately white rabbit twitched his nose and whiskers and flapped his ears forward and back and then to each side in total agreement.

"Doesn't he talk?" asked Josie.

"No," answered Santa. "He's a silent one, he is."

Santa Claus was just as Josie had imagined him to be. He really was a jolly old soul. Josie always wanted to know if it was true that Santa entered homes through their chimneys. Before Josie could put the thought into words, Santa answered with a "Ho, Ho, Ho, my boy. I don't enter a home through its chimney. I enter through the hearts of those who dwell there, and I inspire them to be loving, kind, and giving."

"Do you work with elves?" Josie asked.

"Yes, I do," Santa answered. "I work with an entire team of elves. They help me build goodwill, and sometimes when they feel very creative, they form the goodwill into the shapes of toys. Would you like to meet them?" Josie could hardly believe his good fortune. He followed Santa to a nearby door, decorated with a laurel garland, adorned with multi-colored lights, red ribbons, gingerbread cookies, and candy canes. Santa opened the door, and Josie and Teddy entered his workshop. The room was circular in shape, and there was a raised dais in the center, where the *Naughty and Nice* list sat in its full glory. Josie was tempted to look for his name, to see where he fell in the scheme of things, but he decided not to because he didn't want to appear rude or overly anxious.

Cheerful Christmas tunes played in the background, and Elves sang along while working on their projects. Santa introduced them, one by one, to Teddy and Josie, and Josie was impressed by their delightful sense of humor and positive outlook on life. It was impossible to be in their presence without feeling hopeful, kind, and ever so happy.

Santa then led them to a large red door, and Josie heard the uplifting sound of jingling bells. Santa opened the door and stepped back, revealing the most beautiful reindeer of all standing there in his full glory. Josie gasped aloud, then reached out his hand and touched the deer's velvety nose. Josie was amazed that such a powerful presence could be so gentle and loving. Santa invited the reindeer to join them as they continued exploring the wonders of the workshop. The reindeer was delighted to do so. He walked beside Josie and gave him a soft nuzzle from time to time, leaving Josie with a magical feeling.

The last stop on their tour was the *Wishes Come True* section. It held hundreds of letters addressed to Santa, expressing children's wishes from every part of the world.

"How do you keep up with all of these letters and wishes?" Josie questioned.

"I put them into the *Universe* computer. Every wish that ever came true was processed and delivered by the

Universe. It grants our wishes, every single time, without fail, unless we cancel them."

"Why would someone cancel a wish?"

"There are many factors, but the good news is that once you make a wish, no one else can cancel it. So, you, and only you, are in complete control of whether your wishes come true or not."

Santa suggested that Teddy and Josie pay a visit to the *Universe* computer next. So, they bid Santa, his reindeer, and the elves a fond farewell and continued on their journey. After leaving the workshop, they headed down a long hallway, which led to a spectacular door decorated with every jewel known to man and a few yet to be discovered. Teddy instructed Josie to press a deep blue sapphire lodged in the center of the door. When he did, the door swung open and revealed the strangest computer Josie had ever seen. It was so tall that he could not see the top of it and so long that he couldn't see the end of it. Lights flashed, and buttons clicked as if it was performing a zillion functions all at the same time.

"Would you like to try it?" Teddy asked with a lot of enthusiasm.

"Oh, boy, could I?" Josie responded eagerly.

"Yes, let me explain how it operates," Teddy said while pointing to a stack of paper and a pen sitting on a table in front of the computer.

"First, you write down your wish, and then you slip it into the computer slot marked *Incoming Wishes*, but first you need to..."

Before Teddy could finish his sentence, Josie had already scribbled his wish onto a piece of paper and slipped it into the computer.

"Ut, oh," murmured Teddy, "You should have let me explain everything fully before you did that. There could be serious repercussions if you are not very clear and specific about what you want."

Josie panicked and punched a big red button marked *Cancel*. Then, quick as a flash, a wad of paper, over 30 pounds in weight, flew out of the machine and nearly hit Josie.

"What was that?" he yelled.

"That is one of those repercussions I mentioned. Whenever we react to a situation with fear, the mind takes over, and things tend to grow out of proportion. So it is best to think carefully about what you want before putting in a request and then step back and allow the *Universe* to do its job uninterrupted."

Josie suddenly felt very confused and angry about what had happened. Instantly, without warning, the scenario changed. The two travelers were in a very dark, evil-looking forest. Giant black trees barren of leaves overshadowed them, and horrible sounds filled the dank air. Josie was gripped with terror as he turned to Teddy for an explanation.

"How did we get here?" he hollered.

"Your emotions carried us here," Teddy explained.

"I'm really afraid," cried Josie.

Just then, an ominous-looking black cloud swooshed down to their left, and out of it stepped the most grotesque sight Josie had ever witnessed. It looked like a cross between a witch and a monster. Ten-inch fangs protruded over yellow lips. Dark, matted hair covered the entire body, which was nine feet tall and a bilious green. Growling, snarling sounds poured forth from its throat.

"What is - is that?" Josie stammered while shaking uncontrollably.

"It's a manifestation of your fears," Teddy shouted back over the horrible sounds.

The formidable creature lurched towards them. "Run, Josie, run," Teddy pleaded. And run Josie did, for the longest time, until his legs were exceeding their limits, and tiredness was racking through them.

"I, I can't run anymore," Josie panted.

"Then fly, fly!" hollered Teddy.

"I don't know how to," Josie answered as he collapsed on the ground.

Teddy persisted. "Yes, yes, you do. Flying is a feeling. Remember how you felt when the white stallion took to the air? Recall that feeling and hold on to it!"

Josie tried his best to focus all of his attention on remembering that feeling, but it wasn't easy. The ground shook like thunder as the evil-looking entity gained on them. Josie struggled to his feet, mustered up one final burst of determination, and began to fly. He let out a sigh of relief, and joy coursed through his veins as he felt himself break free of the scene below.

"Look, Teddy!" he exclaimed. "Look how small the monster appears to be from up here."

"Yes, lad," the fairy responded gleefully. "Once we rise above our fears, we realize just how small and insignificant they are."

As Josie soared higher and higher, he felt freer and freer. He looked down once again at the now tiny monster, and it faded away. In its place was Cupid, who was holding a golden bow and an arrow. Cupid pulled back on the string of the bow and released the arrow. It sang out as it flew upward and pierced Josie's heart. Much to Josie's surprise, it didn't hurt. Instead, he was instilled with a great love for all things.

"I'm not hurt," Josie called out to Teddy.

"No, no, of course not. Unconditional love never hurts anyone."

"And I'm flying. How can I fly without wings?"

Teddy smiled, "Your astral body does not need wings to fly. It only needs desire."

Teddy and Josie continued to fly throughout the night. They went up very high, and sometimes they swooped down so low that they could pick violets. They did loop-the-loops and over thirty spins, and they laughed as the flight tickled their very being.

A few hours before dawn, the twosome grew weary from all their adventures. Then, off in the distance, they spotted the *Sound Current* twisting and curving through the night. So, they dove into it and rode the delightful rapids all the way back to Josie's cozy little bedroom just in time to hear the grandfather clock strike five.

CHAPTER 3

THE REALM OF POSSIBILITIES

Mr. MacToodle, the Alester's good neighbor, had three hens and one rooster named George. He was a very old rooster, so he didn't like to rise at dawn to announce the start of the day. He chose instead to sleep in and crow at 7:30 sharp every morning. Josie had a deep love and appreciation for George and visited him every day. He loved the feel of his soft, silky feathers and was mesmerized by his shiny black eyes. Whenever Josie gazed into them, he felt loved and loving.

George crowed five times before Josie heard him that fine morning. Why, if it wasn't for Teddy tugging on his ear, he might not have heard him at all.

"I'm so tired," Josie moaned.

"I understand," Teddy responded. "Facing your fears can be exhausting."

Later that day, a sleepy-eyed Josie sat at his school desk and tried his best to stay alert. Mrs. Cragg passed out new science books and announced the grades from last week's science quiz.

"Josie Alester, C-minus."

"Oh, no," Josie mumbled. "Dad will be so disappointed. I'm no good at science and just look at these new books."

"Why do you find it so difficult?" Teddy asked sympathetically.

"It's boring and confusing. I just can't see it all."

"Would you like to see it all?" Teddy mused with a big grin on his little fairy face. "We could, you know, if you think you're up for another journey tonight."

Josie was definitely ready to embark on another adventure. He felt more confident as a result of what had happened the previous night. He had confronted his fears, risen above them, and survived.

Three rings of the school bell signaled the end of the day. Josie gathered his things and headed for the bus. As he stood in line, he noticed that Kim Starr, the nicest girl in his classroom, was walking towards him. Josie really liked her and hoped that someday she might even be friends with him. His thoughts were suddenly interrupted when Butch deliberately bumped into him.

"Hey, dummy, still talking to fairies?"

Josie spun around, and when he did, the velvet bag came out from under his shirt, catching Butch's attention. Josie quickly grabbed the bag and tucked it back into his shirt.

"What's that?" Butch asked.

"It's a secret," Josie answered.

"Oh, yeah," snipped Butch with a very suspicious look in his eyes. "We'll see."

Josie got on the bus and anxiously awaited his stop. Teddy had missed the entire disturbing event because it was that time of the day when he took his customary nap in Josie's backpack.

Mary Models and Bonji were waiting in the park as usual. But this day, they seemed overly excited about something.

"Josie, Josie," Mary called out. "I have the best news."

Josie ran up to her and bounced Teddy right out of his peaceful sleep.

"What is it, Mary?"

"It's my dream come true - a horse of my very own. He's at the park stable. Come on, let's go."

Josie was very familiar with the park stable. It had two spacious barns, a fenced arena with several jumps placed throughout, and a large grassy pasture. Josie and Mary had spent countless hours riding their imaginary horses around the arena and sailing over low jumps. Excitement welled up inside him as he now imagined doing this on an actual horse.

The two ran joyously toward the stable, with Bonji leaping alongside, barking her approval. Teddy clung to the top of the backpack and grumbled about being so rudely awakened. He wasn't sure what all the fuss was about until they stopped in front of a large box stall. A beautiful chestnut brown horse tossed his proud head and greeted them with a loud whinny. He was indeed a sight to behold, with his black mane and tail, four white markings on his lower legs, and a stark white blaze that ran down the center of his nose.

Josie was jolted out of his reverie when Teddy burst out, "Why, I know that horse. I met him three weeks ago on the *Dream Train*. A more noble beast I've never encountered in all my lives."

"What's his name?" Josie asked aloud.

Mary and Teddy answered simultaneously. Mary said, "I don't know yet," while Teddy said, "San Shrie."

"San Shrie," Josie repeated out loud. The horse immediately shook his head and whinnied. "Gosh," Mary said with astonishment. "How did you come up with that name? He sure seems to like it."

"Oh," said Josie, nervously fumbling for an answer. "Uh, he, ah, looks like a San Shrie, doesn't he?" Then he turned his back to Mary and whispered to Teddy, "Is that really his name?"

"Oh yes," the fairy responded. "It is his spiritual name."

Josie was about to ask Teddy what that meant when Mary shouted out, "Let's ride."

Hours later, a very sore and tired Josie dragged himself home for dinner. He felt so sleepy that he could barely eat. After dismissing dessert, he bathed, retired to his room, and quickly drifted off to sleep. He was abruptly awakened a few hours later by Teddy.

"Wake up, lad, wake up. Did you forget about our journey?"

Josie had indeed forgotten about their plans but had no trouble reviving his spirits when his thoughts turned to the *Dream Train* and a new adventure. He sat up, closed his eyes, and joined Teddy in a Hu song. Within minutes they were aboard the fascinating train and engaged in conversation.

Josie, as usual, had questions.

"What is a spiritual name Teddy?"

"It is a word or sound which resonates with your real self. So, whenever you think of it or sing it like the Hu, it increases your vibratory rate and helps you remember who and what you really are."

"Do I have a spiritual name?" Josie asked.

"Yes, everyone does, even fairies," Teddy answered.

Their conversation was interrupted when the conductor called out, "*Science Museum.*"

The two travelers stepped off the train and saw a beautiful city of lights. It was a remarkable place filled with towering buildings, lots of traffic, and all sorts of creations bustling around.

"Before we visit the museum," Teddy said, "I want to show you the *Astral Library*. Every book that has ever been written or ever will be written is in there."

Josie was expecting the library to be housed in one of the tallest buildings, but Teddy stopped instead in front of a quaint little cottage painted white with green shutters. The windowsills were adorned with flower boxes, filled to the brim with trailing ivy and colorful petunias. There was a simple orange sign hanging above the door with the word *Library* painted on it.

"This is it?" Josie asked in disbelief. "This place doesn't look big enough to be a library."

Teddy chuckled and motioned with his finger for Josie to follow him inside. Once past the door, they entered a massive room filled with books of every size, shape, and color. The room seemed to go on forever and completely baffled Josie's mind. One of its walls was covered with an enormous map of the world. Another wall was painted with famous quotes, and one was constructed entirely of glass and overlooked a river dotted with ships.

"What are those ships doing out there, Teddy?" Josie asked curiously.

"Oh, that is the *Port of Knowledge.* Every ship in the night docks here at one time or another to fill their holds with inspirations."

Josie lingered by the window for a few minutes taking in the enormity of the port and the activity it generated. Next, as he walked up and down aisles of books, Josie noticed sections marked *Past, Present,* and *Future.* He was fascinated by the idea of seeing books from the future, so he headed in that direction. Josie had no sooner arrived when a book flew off its shelf and landed at his feet. He bent over to pick it up and was shocked to see the title "The Adventures of a Spiritual Traveler" and the author "Josie Alester."

"Do you mean," Josie stammered?

"Yes, you will write this book in the future," Teddy replied.

"How?" Josie wondered. "I don't even know what a spiritual traveler is."

"Ho, Ho," Teddy laughed so hard he had to grab his belly to keep it from shaking off.

Josie was fascinated by all of the books and wished he could stay longer, but Teddy reminded him that they needed to move on to the *Science Museum.* Once outside, they followed a pathway lined with lavender, which led to a spectacular rose garden in front of an impressive building looming high up into the sky.

"Is this the museum?" Josie asked.

"Yes," Teddy answered. "It houses every invention of the past, present, and future."

Josie studied the building and noticed that hundreds of marble steps led up to its entrance.

"Oh no," Josie moaned, "It will take us hours to get up those steps."

"No, it won't," Teddy responded. "You can quickly rise to the top by imagining how you will feel when you get there."

Josie imagined himself standing at the top of the steps, feeling relieved and happy, and in the blink of an eye, he was there. He opened an ornately carved wooden door and entered a vast, circular room, which rose fifty stories high. The walls had thousands of carved niches in them, and each one held an invention. A spiraling ramp hugged the walls and was wide enough to accommodate benches where visitors could sit and take in the creative energy. Josie ran up the ramp and went from one captivating invention to another. He was so intrigued that he almost bumped into a young boy.

"Hello," the brown-haired lad said. "My name is Jon Tinker. I am a future scientist, and this is my invention, he said, pointing to a strange-looking item. It is a cathode ray amplifier that will be used by the renowned Joseph Alester."

"My name is Joseph Alester," Josie responded, feeling quite shocked.

"Well, well," Teddy chuckled. "Looks like the cat, or should I say, the future is out of the bag. You two have much to discuss, but not just yet. The great scientists of the world are due here momentarily for a meeting of the minds. We need to quickly descend to the entry-level."

Josie used his newly acquired technique to imagine himself down to the lower level. He could hardly wait to apply this technique to all of his life goals.

The room quickly became so crowded that Josie lost sight of his new acquaintance. The masses moved into the center of the hall, and the walls expanded to accommodate them.

Josie recognized famous individuals from his science books, including Albert Einstein. Teddy had not exaggerated; the great minds were all here. The meeting was brought to order by a tall man in a flowing white robe. He introduced himself as "Sage" and invited everyone to form a circle, join hands, and begin the Hu. As they began to sing, strange but beautiful tones filled the air and merged into one unified sound. At the conclusion of the Hu song, everyone fell silent in preparation for the knowledge they were about to receive. When the contemplative period came to a close, Sage welcomed all and asked if anyone had questions of a spiritual nature. Josie had been meaning to ask Teddy to explain more about vibratory rates, so he decided to seize the opportunity and asked Sage to elaborate.

Sage complied. "Every creation in the physical reality is composed of atoms, which are in a constant state of motion or vibration. An object may appear to be inanimate, like a table or a chair, but at its atomic level, it is in constant motion - vibrating at a particular rate."

"The human body is basically a collection of vibrating atoms. So, when we refer to someone's vibratory rate, we mean the rate at which their collective atoms vibrate. Vibratory rates have a direct correlation to awareness, the higher the vibratory rate, the greater the level of awareness. So, if you want to increase your awareness, you will need to increase your vibratory rate. This can be accomplished by becoming mindful of the places where you spend your time, the company you keep, the things you eat and drink, the music you listen to, the way you spend your time, and even your thoughts and emotions."

"That sounds like a lot of stuff to have to think about," Josie responded.

"Yes," Sage responded. "But the good news is that if you have a strong desire for a high vibratory rate, you will naturally gravitate towards the people, places, and things that support this."

Josie thanked Sage for his wisdom, then returned to his place next to Teddy and reflected on what Sage had shared. Josie didn't like the idea that he might have to give up some of his favorite things so that he could gain more awareness. His mind, being a typical mind, did not like change. So, it felt the need to rebel by filling Josie's thoughts with doubt. "This place isn't real," Josie thought. "Buildings don't grow in size to accommodate the number of people entering them. And how can a huge library fit inside a tiny cottage? Also, it's crazy to think that I am going to become a writer and an inventor. I'm not even that great in school."

Teddy responded in thought, which Josie found to be mildly annoying. "Doubt will not carry you very far in life, Josie. The best destinations are reached by believing that all things are possible."

Josie was still thinking about what he had seen and heard when they returned to the *Dream Train*. His body was tired, but his mind was wide awake and stirred up.

Josie fidgeted in his seat and had trouble settling down.

"Would you like me to tell you a story to help calm your mind?" Teddy asked.

"Oh, yes, please." Josie definitely liked the idea. When he was younger, his mother read him bedtime stories, and he always felt comforted by them.

THE STORY OF POLLY WOLLY

There was a little girl who came to earth from Heaven. Her first name was Polly, and her last name was Wolly. Polly Wolly was always very, very, good except for when she was very, very bad, which, as you know, can happen to the best of us.

Polly had a nightly habit of slipping out of her body as easily as most people slip out of their shoes and clothes. Then she would fly to Heaven to visit her friends. One important thing for you to know is that Polly did not need wings to fly to Heaven. She flew in her dream body instead, which by the way, looked a lot like her earth body, except it never needed to eat or go to the bathroom, and best of all, it never got dirty or had to take a bath.

Some of Polly's friends were in Heaven waiting to be born, while others were simply visiting in their dream bodies. Her very best friend, Little Sky, was always there to greet her when she arrived. Little Sky had previously lived on earth as a Native American girl. When she died and returned to Heaven, she met Polly, who was waiting to be born. They immediately became best friends and remained so even after Polly's birth. Little Sky visited Polly every day using her dream body. Polly could see her as clearly as she could see anyone else on earth. Sadly,

Polly's mother couldn't see her, so she told Polly that Little Sky was imaginary.

Polly would usually leave Heaven, return to her body, wake it up, and use it all day long. But one night, she decided to leave her body behind for good because she was all finished with it and was ready for something new. When she shared the news with Little Sky, the two friends were so happy that they jumped up and down and hugged and giggled. Then they flew around and around before landing on a soft cloud to tickle their tummies.

Time, as we know it in the physical reality, doesn't exist in Heaven. Years of physical time can pass in the blink of an eye in Heaven, so those who dwell there don't miss the loved ones they leave behind. There is no need to because they know they will reunite with them in one or two blinks of an eye. They do, however, have moments of concern for their loved ones, so Little Sky was not surprised at all when Polly said, "I am worried about my mother. It's been a long time in physical terms since I died. I know that she must be missing me, and I don't want her to feel lonely or sad."

"Your mother is still sleeping," Little Sky responded. "Let's go visit her in a dream."

"Oh, that would be fun!" Polly laughed. But then Polly quickly lost her enthusiasm as she remembered that grown-ups don't usually remember their inner dream lives because they are so focused on their outer day-to-day lives.

Polly nodded her head solemnly since she knew this to be true.

Polly and Little Sky decided to visit Polly's mother anyway, and it turned out to be one of Polly's mother's best dreams. Polly told her all about Heaven and how happy she was. She shared that someday they would get to be in Heaven together and live happily ever after in their dream bodies if they wanted to. Polly's mother laughed and then cried.

"Why are you crying, Mommy?" Polly asked.

"Because this is just a dream, and you aren't really here."

Polly barely had enough time to give her mother one brief, loving kiss on the cheek before they faded from her memory.

The two friends found themselves back in Heaven again and were wondering what they should do when Little Sky's brother, Bouncing Bear, came bouncing along with a great idea.

"Let's go and visit God," he said enthusiastically.

So, off they went, partly flying and partly running, all the way to God's mighty throne, which was surrounded by hundreds of baby angels known as Cherubs. Most of the cherubs had tiny wings, but a few didn't have any at all. Polly found this confusing, and she asked Little Sky if she knew why.

"Some cherubs don't have wings because they would interfere with their mission," Little Sky explained. "Wingless cherubs are sent to earth disguised as human babies. They come to earth as babies, die soon thereafter, and then fly very quickly back to Heaven. They only stay long enough to plant the seeds of God's love in the hearts of those they touch. Then they return home, sit beside God and watch the seeds of love grow and take hold for all of eternity. When someone has been graced with the presence of a cherub, they are never the same again."

Angelic music could be heard as Polly, Little Sky, and Bouncing Bear approached God's throne. Little Sky wanted to sit on God's knee, and Polly wanted to touch God's golden crown, so of course, God let them. Bouncing Bear just stood off to the side and watched silently because little boys don't care about all that stuff. They just want to feel loved.

Before long, children of all types, shapes, and colors began arriving at the throne and were welcomed by God. As dawn slowly approached the earth, the children grew very sleepy, so they snuggled up next to puppy dogs and kittens waiting to be born and dreamt sweet dreams of beautiful things to come.

———————————

Josie felt much calmer at the story's end but wondered aloud if God actually existed.

"God does exist but doesn't always sit on a throne in Heaven," Teddy responded.

"Where else can I find God?"

"Everywhere, Josie, everywhere."

"Can I meet God?" Josie asked in a reverent tone.

"You can not only meet God," Teddy answered. "You can come to know God as well as you know yourself."

Josie let out a big sigh of relief, closed his eyes, and went to sleep.

CHAPTER 4

THE GATES OF HEAVEN

A familiar voice pierced the stillness. "Josie, darling, it's past eight. You'll miss the bus."

Josie recognized his mother's voice and forced his eyelids to open.

"Eight?" He yawned. "I must have forgotten to set my alarm, and I didn't even hear George crow."

"Nevertheless," Mrs. Alester admonished. "You have overslept. Now hurry, please."

Once she was out of earshot, Josie turned to Teddy, "Did you hear George crow?"

"No, I didn't, Josie, because George didn't crow this morning. Nor will he crow ever again."

"Why not?" Josie asked.

Teddy looked compassionately at Josie and said, "Because he died last night."

"George died?" Josie asked in disbelief. "I loved George, even when I would get upset with him for waking me up on the weekends. I loved him, and I didn't get to tell him. I didn't even get to say goodbye."

"Goodbye?" Teddy asked. "Why would you say goodbye at a time like this?"

"I don't understand," Josie said, wiping another tear with the back of his hand.

"Goodbye means bye for good," Teddy continued. "George isn't gone for good. His body might not be alive, but the rest of him is very much alive and well and living on the *Astral*. Oh dear, I can tell we need to make another trip to clear things up for you. We'll talk later. Dry your tears and get dressed so we won't miss the bus."

Much to Mrs. Alester's relief, Josie and Teddy did not miss the bus that morning. However, it wasn't long before Josie wished they had. Butch Kellog was determined to make Josie's red velvet pouch his own and had devised a plan to get it. He waited until the bus pulled up in front of the school, then strutted down the bus's aisle and pretended to trip. He fell against Josie and, with one quick jerk, yanked the gold chain off of Josie's neck.

"Ooof," Teddy bellowed. "He nearly crushed me."

Josie looked at Teddy and inspected the little man for injuries.

"That rotten Butch," Josie said. "He hurt my neck."

Josie felt his neck and screamed, "The special dust, Teddy, it's gone!"

Before Josie could get up, Butch jumped off the bus and ran away. Josie pushed his way to the front and went after him in hot pursuit.

"Over there," Teddy shouted from his perch on Josie's shoulder. "I see him behind the dumpster."

Josie raced over to the dumpster and surprised Butch, who had squatted down to examine the contents of the mysterious bag. Startled by Josie's sudden appearance, Butch jumped up and tossed the stolen goods into the air. The precious dust fell out and blew away in one puff of wind. Butch panicked and ran off, leaving Josie to recover the empty pouch and broken chain.

"Oh no," Josie moaned. "The dust. It's gone. What an awful day this has been - first George, now this." He wanted to cry so badly that he had to swallow hard to restrain his tears. Crying at home in the privacy of his bedroom was one thing but crying in front of his schoolmates was quite another. It would just be too embarrassing. Josie fought hard, but a lone, determined tear found its way to the corner of his eye and rolled down his cheek. A very compassionate Teddy reached over and dabbed it away with his teensy, tiny handkerchief.

"There, there lad, lighten your heart. You needn't be concerned about the loss of your treasure."

"What do you mean?" Josie stammered. "It was magic. I need it to solve my problems and to feel happy."

"No, no," Teddy answered reassuringly. "The dust wasn't magic, and you don't need it to solve your problems or to feel happy. It was just a reminder of the answers you already have within you - answers that come to us when we believe they can and will. Feeling happy, on the other hand, is something that requires commitment and practice."

"How do I practice feeling happy?" Josie asked.

"Well, you begin by remembering a time when you felt very happy," Teddy explained.

"I remember feeling very happy when I went to the amusement park," Josie replied.

"OK. Now close your eyes, imagine you are back at the amusement park, and remember what that felt like."

"How can I feel it without actually being at the amusement park?" Josie asked.

"Because happiness is not a place or an event. It's a decision. You decide to be happy, and when you do, everything in the *Universe* will line up to support that decision. Then before you know it, you will feel happy. However, if you are not in the habit of feeling happy, this can slow down the process considerably. So, let's get back to the task at hand. Remember what happiness felt like both emotionally and physically. For example, when I am happy, I feel good and kind and loving. My tummy feels as if it has butterflies in it, and the rest of my body feels as light as a feather."

"Yes," Josie said in agreement. "It feels good all over. It just feels right, like how I am always meant to be."

"OK, then." Teddy continued. "Memorize that feeling. Practice feeling it over and over throughout your day until it becomes second nature, and you can draw upon it at will."

Josie's happiness decision was sorely tested that day. Each time he thought about losing George, he felt a pain deep inside his chest, and tears welled up in his eyes. Josie also felt guilty, trying to be happy when George had just died. He wondered if being happy at a time like this would mean that he didn't really miss George or care about him. So when the bell rang for recess, Josie didn't join his schoolmates. Instead, he walked over to a bench away from the play area, cried a few tears, and shared his thoughts with Teddy.

Teddy gave Josie a comforting hug and said, "You feel this way because you're in the habit of thinking that outer events can or should make you happy or sad. Nothing in creation can make you feel happy or sad. You and only you get to decide how you are going to feel at any given moment. Once true happiness has firmly taken hold in your heart, you will be able to connect with it at any time, even if you are sad and crying."

The school bell rang out, signaling the end of recess, and Josie returned to his classroom with a heavy heart. He felt confused about some of the things Teddy had shared, and his mind was growing weary. Josie was looking forward to bedtime, so he could sleep and escape the day. Teddy, on the other hand, was planning the perfect remedy for Josie's dilemma. He allowed Josie to sleep for a few hours and then gently whispered into his ear, "Would you like to visit George?" Josie quickly sat up and eagerly agreed to another journey. A short while later, the two spiritual travelers rode in contemplative silence on the now-familiar train.

Josie was deep in thought about the things Teddy had shared earlier when the train drew to a stop. He stepped off the train and found himself at the edge of what appeared to be an endless desert.

"This is the biggest desert I have ever seen," Josie commented while trudging along.

"My dear lad, what you see here is not a desert," Teddy replied. "It is the *Sands of Time*. Every grain of sand holds a past, present, or future memory."

Crossing the *Sands of Time* was Josie's most fascinating journey yet. Each grain had a different story to tell, one more interesting than the other. Josie wanted to listen to them all, but they reached a fenced garden, and Teddy explained that the sands were not permitted inside.

"What is this place?" Josie asked.

"This is Heaven," Teddy responded with a glimmer in his eyes.

Heaven's gates were made of pure gold. They were very tall and very wide and incredibly beautiful. Angels were standing just inside, along with a few people who looked as if they were waiting for someone. A moment later, a man walked past Teddy and Josie and approached the gates. He was moving at such a slow pace and looked so exhausted that Josie wasn't sure if he would make it all the way there. An angel glided towards him and spread her wings open, displaying their full glory. Then she took the man's hands in hers, and they floated effortlessly towards Heaven. Once inside, he was greeted by loved ones who had been waiting patiently for him. They embraced him and welcomed him home, and he became energized and reassured by their presence.

Josie then noticed a group of people standing outside the gates with looks of shame on their faces. They seemed to be suffering and in pain.

"Are those the people who aren't good enough to get into Heaven?" Josie asked.

"The gates of Heaven are never closed to anyone. All are welcome inside at any time," Teddy answered. "These individuals are not entering because they don't think they deserve Heaven and believe that they should be punished for their sins."

"Are they going to be punished?" Josie asked.

"No. Not at all," Teddy responded. "The pain and suffering they are experiencing are entirely self-inflicted. They don't realize that they aren't bad people. They were simply lost, confused, and trapped in a physical life that was lacking in love. This is never a cause for punishment. No need to worry, though. The healing energy emanating from Heaven will eventually draw them inside the gates, and they will see their spiritual perfection reflected in the beauty of the garden."

"Let's go inside," Teddy suggested.

"Go in," Josie responded in confusion. "We can't go in. We're not dead yet."

Teddy let out a giggle. "We don't have to be dead to experience Heaven, laddie. We are free to do that at any given moment."

Josie was amazed as they ventured into the sacred garden. It was so quiet and peaceful that Teddy spoke in hushed tones. "This is the *Garden of the Souls*. Every soul spends time here between lives. It is a place for rest, healing, contemplation, and rejuvenation."

The garden held every tree, shrub, flower, and grass in creation. Some areas were perfectly manicured, while others were left to their own wild imaginations. Josie followed a series of stepping-stones, which led to a lovely pond filled with bright koi fish. Some were darting back and forth, making ripples in the water, while others were resting in the shade of a flowering cherry tree. Teddy pointed towards a sign with the word *Transition* carved into it. They headed in that direction and passed by a group of people moving in complete silence. Some were confused about where they were because they hadn't previously believed in a life after death. Others were delighted that the afterlife was even more incredible than they thought it would be. Teddy explained that this section of the garden was designed to help souls transition from the *Physical* realm to life in another realm.

Cozy lounge chairs were parked in the shade of mighty oaks, and people of all types were resting on them. A few looked as if they were taking a refreshing nap, while others seemed to be in a state of deep sleep. Teddy explained that some lifetimes are more traumatic than others and require a greater rest and recovery period.

Josie was impressed by the number and variety of animals that he saw in Heaven. Horses of every breed and color were stretched out on the ground, sleeping soundly in the sunlight. Several antelope and llamas were grazing on lush patches of grass while colorful birds flew above, and a chubby panda bear rolled down a hill with a wide grin on its face.

"I didn't know that animals lived in Heaven," Josie said.

"It wouldn't be Heaven without them," Teddy chuckled in response.

The two travelers followed a winding trail, which led to an ivy-covered building that seemed older than time itself.

"Where are we?" Josie asked.

"This is the *Hall of Akashic Records*. It contains detailed records of the past, present, and future of every life form."

"Even me?"

"Yes, lad. Every one of your lives, both the good and the not so good, are recorded here."

"Kind of like a *Naughty and Nice* list?" Josie commented.

"Similar," Teddy replied. "But this list doesn't earn us coal in our stockings or gifts under the tree. Our accumulated experiences are referred to as karma. We carry our karma from one lifetime to another, so we can draw upon those experiences to assist us with our spiritual growth."

"The same way I carry the knowledge of one plus one equals two, from one grade to the next?"

"Exactly, lad."

"Do we have lots of lives?" Josie asked.

"Yes, because soul is always seeking knowledge and wants to experience things from all perspectives."

On the outside, the hall didn't seem that big. But, on the inside, it was beyond measure. Josie saw people sitting silently at long tables, reviewing large, leather-bound books that contained their records.

"Can I read my record?" Josie asked Teddy.

"Yes, of course. You are welcome to do that at any time, but tonight we'd best focus on our visit with George."

Teddy directed Josie into a busier part of the building. The area was filled with so many windows that it boggled the imagination. Some were wide open. Some were closed shut, and others were at various stages in between. All types of beings were coming and going through the windows.

"What's that all about?" a perplexed Josie asked Teddy.

"These are spiritual windows, portals between the *Astral* and *Physical* realms. When someone is ready to leave the *Astral* to be born in the *Physical*, a spiritual window opens to accommodate the transition. A window also opens at the time of death to facilitate a return to the *Astral*. Once a window has opened, it takes about two weeks to close again in physical reality time. During this period, loved ones of the deceased, who are still in the *Physical*, can use the window to bring new experiences into their lives and to release those they no longer wish to have."

"So, a window opened when George died?"

"Yes, it did."

"Which one?"

"I'm not certain."

"Well, how will I know which one to use to get rid of my old situations and bring in new ones?"

"You don't have to know. You just need to sit down and write a list of the things you want to release and the things you want to bring in. The *Universe* computer will take it from there. However, it will only work if you are truly committed to a change. The human mind is known for saying it wants one thing when it is actually committed to something else entirely."

Teddy suggested that they move on lest they should miss seeing George. He directed Josie to another section of the building, which was also bustling with activity. Signs indicating various life categories were suspended above a counter, and beings were lined up beneath in wait. Josie looked to Teddy for clarity.

"These individuals are waiting to be reborn into the *Physical*. This process is called reincarnation, and it begins with making a detailed list of the experiences one wishes to have in a new life. Next, the list goes into the *Universe* computer. Then, it scans for all possible matches, considering particulars such as the time and location of birth, sex, type of species, and many other factors. In the case of a human incarnation, the computer also considers the family the human will be born into, the person's race, body type and condition, sexual orientation, and so on. The computer then comes up with a suggested life, but everyone has the free will to accept or reject a proposal. No one is ever thrust into a life that they haven't chosen and agreed to."

Teddy then led Josie to a sign at the far end of the room, which read *Transmigration.*

"What's transmigration?" Josie wanted to know.

"It's what happens when you are done experiencing a particular physical form and are ready to incarnate as a different one. For example, let's say that you spent many lifetimes as a duck, and now you want to experience life as an elephant. You can choose to transmigrate from duck form to elephant form or even human form."

"Wow! You mean I could have been a duck in a previous life?"

"Yes, or you might be a duck in a future life."

The two hurried over to the transmigration area and found themselves in the midst of a group of beings who were bristling with excitement. They edged their way up to the front, and lo and behold, there stood George, the Rooster.

"George!" Josie exclaimed joyously. George turned, and upon seeing his favorite human, he crowed, not one, not two, but three long, delicious crows. Josie embraced his friend lovingly and almost cried with joy.

"I thought I'd never see you again," Josie began. "When I heard that you had died, I...."

"Oh, that," George interrupted. "Funny how quickly you can forget a little thing like that."

"Little thing!" Josie exclaimed.

"Little, compared to what's ahead. My next life will not be in rooster form, and from the looks of things, it is going to be a humdinger!"

George stepped up to the clerk and introduced himself, "Past life name, George Rooster. Spiritual name, Ray Don Sisk."

The clerk smiled and asked George if he had received the computer's life suggestions. George indicated that he had and was ready to move forward. Next, the clerk handed him a portfolio, which contained a detailed outline of George's karma.

"Review it carefully, for as you know, the birth process can cause a bit of amnesia. You may now proceed to the *Mission* area to receive your assignment."

Josie whispered to Teddy, "What's a mission?"

"When we are granted a new life, we are also assigned a mission that we must complete in exchange."

"Is everyone given a mission?"

"Yes, and everyone's mission is the same. It is to deliver a special gift to the *Physical*."

"So, I have a mission, a gift to deliver?"

"Yes, laddie, you do."

"But I don't remember what it is."

"Your mission will be revealed to you in time if you do something you absolutely love to do every single day, something that makes you feel bouncing off the walls happy."

"What happens if we don't remember our mission?" Josie inquired. "Does the mission get assigned to someone else?"

"No, it doesn't because just as every being is unique, the way they deliver the gift is also unique. You know how there can be many singers who sing the same song? The words of the song might be the same, but each singer delivers them in a unique way. The same holds true of gift bearers. So, if someone fails to deliver a gift, this is a tragic loss for all involved because the delivery of a gift is as important as the gift itself."

Just then, George turned to Josie and gave him a warm, loving hug with his rooster wings. "I have to go now," he said to Josie with a smile on his face. "I have much to do in preparation for my next life."

"Will I ever see you again?" Josie asked.

"Oh yes, and then some," George laughed."

"I love you, George," Josie stammered. "And I always did."

"I love you too," George answered. "And I always will."

George walked off, waving to Josie and Teddy. Josie cupped his hands around his mouth and shouted, "How will I find you?"

"I'll find you," George hollered back.

"But how will I know you?" Josie stammered with a tear in his eye.

"You'll know," George crowed. "You'll know." And with that, he was gone, and Josie felt sad for himself.

Teddy resumed his customary position of sitting on Josie's left shoulder. "Would you like to look around some more?" he asked.

"No," Josie answered, "Not tonight. Can we go home? I suddenly have a longing for it."

Teddy smiled with a look of wisdom and granted Josie's wish.

CHAPTER 5

THE MENTAL REALM

Josie was grateful that it was Saturday. He felt like he had a lot to reflect on, so he decided to spend a quiet day at home and read a good book. His bedroom chair was roomy and cozy. It was perfect for curling up on with the snuggly afghan his mother had lovingly crocheted for him. Teddy was nestled nearby in his cigar box bed, contemplating and giving thanks for his many blessings.

Josie chose a book about a ghost horse who manifested in the *Physical* to help a young boy regain his confidence. Josie was curious about the nature of ghosts, so he asked Teddy if he could enlighten him. Of course, Teddy was happy to oblige.

"A ghost is a spirit who died while in the *Physical* and then returned to the *Astral* without a physical body. The *Astral* is separated from the *Physical* by a thin veil of energy. At the time of death, the spirit passes through this veil and enters the lowest level of the *Astral*, which is filled with darkness. The highest level of the *Astral* is Heaven, which is filled with light. Typically, when a spirit crosses into the darkness of the lower *Astral*, the light from Heaven draws them rapidly towards it. However, a spirit can linger in the lower *Astral* for many reasons. For example, if death was very sudden, the spirit might not realize it has occurred. Or a spirit can have a strong attachment to life in the *Physical*, a feeling of unfinished business, or a concern for loved ones left behind. In these situations, spirits might wander back and forth between the *Physical* and the *Astral,* attempting to communicate with those still living in the *Physical* or due to a desire to participate in a physical life again. Disembodied spirits can cause physical noises, manipulate physical objects, and even appear as an orb, shadow, or shape. However, these manifestations cannot occur unless the spirit has a source of emotional energy to fuel them. These sources can include physical beings who are hyperactive, despondent, suffering from an addiction, or experiencing a highly emotional state, such as grieving a loved one's death. Fear is also a great source of energy, which is why some spirits move objects or make eerie noises to frighten people. Loved ones can also hold a spirit back if their grief or attachment to the deceased is strong enough. For this reason, it is important to release any attachments we may have to our departed loved ones, so they can feel free to enjoy the wonderful afterlife, which they so richly deserve. We might miss them, but we can take comfort in the fact that the time we spend with our loved ones, while in the *Physical,* is brief compared to the time we will spend with them throughout eternity."

"The horse in the book you are reading is not an actual ghost. It is a highly evolved spirit guide who can manifest as a horse or as any other lifeform to aide those in need."

Josie wondered if he would someday be fortunate enough to have a spirit guide of his very own. Teddy quietly chuckled and shook his head.

Josie soon grew very sleepy and dozed off. He immediately found himself on the *Dream Train,* sitting next to Teddy. Josie looked out the window but could not see anything. Up to now, all of Josie's journeys on the train had been filled with light. This was the first time they had traveled in darkness.

"Where are we going," Josie asked?

"Well, since we were discussing the lower *Astral* today, I thought it would be an opportune time to visit it."

The train seemed to groan to a stop, and when they stepped off, a one-legged raven, with a peg leg and a black patch covering his right eye, swooped low over Josie and cawed, "Beware the mental trap. Beware the mental trap." And then, with a loud clap of his dark wings, he was gone.

"The mental trap?" Josie repeated with a half-frightened, half-puzzled look on his face.

"Ah, yes," Teddy mused. "Mental traps are horrible, dangerous, and swift. But we will try our best to avoid them."

"Gosh, Teddy, I'm not sure I want to be here. It sounds scary."

"Have no fear, my boy," the little man answered. "It isn't any scarier than your own mentalizing can make it."

"Mentalizing, what's that?" Josie asked, looking over his shoulder nervously.

"Mentalizing is when you become so afraid or worried that you allow your mind to take over your thoughts."

The two adventurers trudged along for quite some time before approaching an intimidating black castle. It was surrounded by a tall stone wall with sharp metal spikes protruding from the top. Everything about it was repulsive, but for some reason, Josie felt strangely drawn to it.

"What is this place?" Josie asked Teddy.

"This is the home of Maya, queen of illusion. Her job is to keep spiritual beings trapped in darkness by creating illusions that make situations seem worse than they are. Another of her favorite illusions is to make it appear as if escape from a situation is hopeless. You must remember when faced with a seemingly hopeless situation that nothing is ever as bad as it seems, and there is always a way out if you believe there is."

As frightened as Josie was, he still found the Castle hard to resist.

"I wish we could see what's on the other side of the wall," Josie said.

"We can," Teddy said while pushing his body right through the brick wall until Josie could no longer see him. Teddy then withdrew it just as effortlessly.

"You see, Josie, it isn't a real wall. It is merely an illusion, like everything else here."

Josie wanted to get a closer look at the castle, so he pushed his head through the wall with so much enthusiasm that his whole body went through. He was amazed and intrigued by what he saw. Everything seemed devoid of life. The trees and flowers were black and drooping as if carrying a heavy burden. The air felt thick, and breathing was difficult. A small part of Josie wanted to leave, but a greater part of him wanted to stay. He felt compelled to enter the castle and take in its energy.

Teddy had previously taught Josie that it was essential to remain positive at all times. Josie often found this challenging to do, whereas being negative felt like second nature. Negativity was as cozy as slipping into an old pair of bedroom slippers that were not very pretty to look at but oh so comfortable. The deeper Josie ventured into the castle, the better he felt about being negative. He started to recall all the mean things that others had done to him. He thought of Butch in particular. Josie wanted to get back at Butch - hurt him somehow. The more he thought about it, the more he resented Butch. It didn't take long for his resentment to grow into pure hatred. Josie was very familiar with being negative, but he had never before experienced full-blown hatred for someone. It didn't feel good at all. He felt sick to his stomach and began having concerns for his well-being. Josie wanted to run away, but the pull he felt from the castle was so strong that he couldn't move his feet.

"Ha, ha, ha, ha," a voice cackled out of the darkness.

Josie strained his eyes to see who or what it was. "Who's there?" he yelled out.

The one-eyed raven he had encountered at the train station swooped down over his head. Josie's fears suddenly got the best of him. The floor beneath him opened up, and he was cast down into a deep, dark dungeon. The only visible light came from a candle sconce on the wall.

Josie felt a flutter of wings and knew that the raven had followed him into the dungeon. "Can you help me?" Josie pleaded.

"No. Nope. Negative," the raven responded. "Nobody can help you, but you, you, you."

"What is this place?" Josie asked.

"It's a mind trap," the raven answered. "A purely self-inflicted mind trap. Now you are all alone with what you've invented." Josie felt one final swoosh of wings, and POOF, the crow was gone.

"All alone?" a bewildered Josie said aloud. He quickly looked around for Teddy, but alas, it was true. Josie was all alone. He had been so caught up in the spell of the castle that he had forgotten entirely about Teddy. Josie frantically looked around for a door, a window, or some sign of hope, but there wasn't any. Finally, he sank onto the damp floor, buried his face in his hands, and began to cry. Josie wondered what would become of him. "Why?" Josie yelled out in anger and frustration. "Why did this happen to me? Why do bad things keep happening to me? I'm a good person. Why am I being punished?" Josie jumped up and punched the wall but only hurt himself more. He continued crying for a long time, and then when he couldn't cry anymore, he just gave up, sat down in defeat, and surrendered to the situation. Eventually, this led to him feeling a little restless but not enough to provoke an action. It reminded Josie of how he felt when he was bored. Yes, that was it. He was beginning to become bored with the situation. The boredom grew more and more with each passing moment and eventually became so overwhelming that Josie just had to get up and do something. First, he examined the entire dungeon once again for cracks, doors, or windows, in case he had missed them the first time he looked. Next, he decided to mentally review the steps he had taken that landed him in the dungeon. He realized that things went terribly wrong as soon as he started to mentalize. Perhaps, he had even unknowingly fallen under one of Maya's spells.

He wondered where Teddy was. He deeply missed him. A spark of hope glimmered in Josie's mind as he thought of the fairy dressed in blue. "What was it that he told me never to forget?" Instantly, the answer came. "You must remember when faced with a seemingly hopeless situation that nothing is ever as bad as it seems, and there is always a way out if you believe there is."

Josie felt that his plight could definitely be categorized as seemingly hopeless, so he applied Teddy's advice to the problem. "Escape from this dungeon is not as hopeless as it seems," he said aloud. "I believe there is a way out." Just then, a door appeared in front of Josie and swung open. Teddy was standing on the other side and greeted Josie with a warm hug.

"Hurry, boy," he cautioned. "We are not out of danger yet. The negative forces are after you."

"But why?" asked Josie.

"Why?" Teddy answered. "Because you discovered the secret escape route from a mind trap, that's why. They don't want you sharing that knowledge with anyone else."

Josie heard footsteps running behind him.

"Here they come," cried Teddy. "Run. Run."

Josie did not mentalize this time. He heard and sensed the danger and ran as fast as he could.

"Go in there," Teddy directed, pointing to a dark tunnel. "The *Dream Train* is due momentarily. We'll be safe there."

Josie heeded Teddy's direction but stopped when he reached the tunnel opening because the train lights were now visible and heading straight for them.

"Leap into the tunnel," Teddy yelled. "It is your only hope, lad."

"I -- I can't," cried Josie. "I'm afraid that the train will run us over."

"Quit mentalizing, Josie. Leap!"

The negative forces were closing in on Josie. He could feel their cold breath on his back. In a final act of desperation, Josie heeded Teddy's direction, closed his eyes, and leaped right into the train. And then an incredible thing happened. Josie felt as if he was the train itself, with all of its thundering power and potential. Josie then experienced a peace he had never felt before, and it left him with a longing to have it again.

CHAPTER 6

THE DARK NIGHT OF SOUL

The following day, Josie asked Teddy why the *Dream Train* had seemed so threatening when he had to decide between it and the negative forces. Teddy explained that Maya had cast a spell on Josie to make the safety of the train appear more frightening than the negative forces who were after him.

Josie was relieved that he had escaped the lower *Astral* and was now safely back in the *Physical*. What he didn't realize was that Maya's grasp was so far-reaching that it extended into the *Physical* and allowed her to cast a spell on anyone who dwelled there.

Mrs. Alester drove Josie to school that day because she was going right past it on her way to visit a friend. Josie was relieved that he didn't have to ride on the bus with Butch. His body felt icky, and his mind felt angry. Josie knew that he should focus on being positive by making a happiness decision, but he didn't want to. He just wanted to feel sorry for himself. Once in that state, it didn't take long for Josie to become completely engulfed in negativity. He started feeling that life, in general, was unfair. Then he began to focus on the things he didn't like about his school, teacher, and classmates. Eventually, his negative thoughts spread to his parents and, above all, to Teddy. Josie reflected on the days when he would sit in school and think about having fun with his friends. Then Teddy entered his life, and all Josie thought about was making happiness decisions, discovering his mission, delivering his gift to the world, writing a book, and inventing something. It seemed like he was under a lot of pressure to grow up and show up. Josie didn't like this. He thought, "I'm just a kid. I shouldn't have to be so responsible." After considerable contemplation, Josie decided, "I don't care about true happiness anymore. Plain old happiness is fine with me. So, I'm just going to focus on that." Josie was so caught up in Maya's spell that he didn't notice a discomfort growing in his heart. He also didn't notice how very silent Teddy had become.

Josie headed for the stables after school and was looking forward to riding. Mary mounted San Shrie when she saw Josie approaching. They were in the habit of riding double, alternating between sitting in the saddle and riding behind it. It was Mary's turn to ride in the saddle. She rode up to Josie and reached down to help him up. As soon as he put his foot in the stirrup, San Shrie snorted and stepped aside. Mary tried two more times with the same result. "San Shrie," Mary called out, "What is wrong with you? Why won't you stand still and let Josie on?" San Shrie responded with a whinny so shrill that it almost shook Mary off. "I don't know what's wrong," Mary said. "Maybe he doesn't feel well. I don't think we should try riding him today."

Mary didn't realize that San Shrie was reacting to Josie's negative state. Horses are masters at reading energy and always resist when asked to do something, which is not in the best interest of the whole.

Mary invited Josie to come to her house instead and play a board game, but Josie declined, saying that he was tired. The truth was that he just wanted to be left alone so that he could feel sorry for himself in the privacy of his own mind.

Josie and Teddy barely spoke a word that evening. Josie felt relieved when he finally turned out the light to go to sleep, and the awkward silence between them ended. When Josie awoke the following day, he was glad that it was Saturday so he could lie in bed and contemplate on his situation. He felt a lot of anger - first towards San Shrie for depriving him of the fun of riding and secondly towards Teddy. "Things were more fun before Teddy showed up with the blue dust," Josie thought. "Maybe I should ask Teddy to go away." The more he thought about it, the better it sounded. "Yes," he decided, "I will definitely ask Teddy to leave as soon as I get up." Well, as we all know, sometimes even our best plans fail us, and

Josie thought for sure that this was one of his best plans. Little did he know that Teddy had already packed up the pajamas and pillow Josie made for him, hopped onto an early morning sunbeam, and quietly disappeared.

Josie was stirred out of his reverie when a piece of paper drifted down and brushed by his nose. It was a note from Teddy.

Dear Josie,

I came into your life because of a wish you made for help. Now, I am leaving due to your wish for me to be gone from your life. I am most grateful for the time and the love we have shared, and I treasure the memories of the incredible journeys we have taken. I will always hold you in my thoughts and in my heart.

I wish you much love and many blessings,

Teddy

Mixed emotions overtook Josie and spread confusion through his mind. He spent the entire weekend not knowing if he should feel happy or sad. On the one hand, he was delighted to focus exclusively on fun, but on the other hand, he felt a certain emptiness without Teddy.

Josie was still feeling conflicted when he met up with Mary after school. She was standing next to San Shrie's stall with no intention of riding him that day.

Instead, she took Josie by the hand and told him that she had something wonderful to show him back at her house. Josie reluctantly went along, not even caring what it was. When they arrived at her home, Mary led him to a large dog bed in the corner of the living room. He looked down and saw Bonji with five tiny newborn puppies curled up next to her tummy. "Wow," Josie exclaimed, "When did this happen?"

"Last night," Mary answered.

"Aren't they the best - the best things you have ever seen?" Mary asked with pride.

Josie had to think hard before answering because he had seen so many amazing things on his travels with Teddy.

"They are like a little slice of Heaven," Josie finally responded.

That night, a heavy-hearted Josie climbed into bed, wondering if the *Dream Train* would come, but it never did. Instead, he had a restless night, filled with disturbing dreams and unsettling feelings.

The next day was the last school day before summer break. When the bell rang out for recess, Josie's classmates spilled out into the playground, eager to share their plans for the summer. Josie did not join them. He chose instead to sit on a bench and nurse his growing depression. His thoughts were interrupted by a soft, gentle voice saying,

"Hello." Josie looked up and was surprised to see Kim Starr standing there in front of him.

"Hhhi, hi," Josie stammered.

"Where's your fairy today?" Kim asked.

Josie was shocked. "What? You saw him?" Josie asked with a tremor in his voice.

"Of course."

Josie sat there with his mouth wide open, not knowing what to say. Kim waited for a response, and when she didn't get one, she bent down to pluck a wild daisy growing out of a crack in the play yard. A small red velvet bag, suspended on a gold chain, swung out of her blouse and glimmered in the sunlight. Josie jumped up. "What is that?"

Kim lifted the chain as she answered, "This was a hello gift from my fairy guide, Melina." Just then, as if summoned, Melina appeared in front of Josie and waved. Josie stood in stunned silence, not knowing how to respond. When the school bell rang out to signal the end of recess, his mind clicked back into gear, yet he was still at a loss for words. Kim handed the daisy to Josie and said, "We better get back to class," before running off with Melina flying beside her.

Throughout the remainder of the day, Josie's mind raced back and forth between confusion, sadness, and a slight spark of happiness. He went straight home after school and retired to his room to reflect on what had transpired. Josie missed Teddy, but at the same time, he resented him for stirring up his life. Josie thought about the times he felt overwhelmed and afraid during their travels together, but then, there was good stuff too. Josie loved flying, the way he felt when Cupid shot him, and his visit to Santa's workshop. He had learned so much yet also felt burdened at times by the responsibility of the knowledge. Josie reviewed the high and low points of a life with Teddy for a long time and eventually grew so weary of the internal conflict that he surrendered to the fact that Teddy was gone, and there didn't seem to be anything he could do about it. So, he decided to stay true to his course of just having fun!

Josie started spending most of his free time with friends, who were also committed to having fun, even if it was at the expense of others. He no longer cared about anyone's feelings except his own. He grew more selfish and less aware with each passing day. Josie was even glad when Mary left and went to her Grandmother's farm for the summer with the puppies and San Shrie in tow. Mary was a constant reminder of what it felt like to focus on love and kindness, and he decided that it was a reminder he didn't need or want.

As the weeks passed by, Josie started to feel a greater sense of freedom since Teddy's departure, but he never felt truly happy. At one point, he thought about Bonji's puppies and wondered if a puppy would be fun to have. So, Josie asked his parents if he could have one when they were old enough to leave Bonji. They said yes, but only if Josie promised that he would take care of it every day. Josie thought this over and decided that taking care of a puppy would be too much work and not worth the effort.

The days grew into weeks and the weeks into months. Josie started to feel lost, then absolutely stuck in place. He did not have a clear direction about how to move forward. Life was no longer shiny and bright. Everything looked gloomy and hopeless as Josie sank into a deep, dark depression. He began to spend most of his free time at home, grateful that school was out for the summer. He slept a lot and watched TV, and even though he wasn't very active, he felt exhausted at the end of each day. One night as he was lying in bed, he felt so awful that he silently reached out for help. He barely remembered doing this as he drifted off to sleep.

CHAPTER 7

THE INNER MASTER

A soft musical sound awakened Josie. "Was it violins?" he wondered. "No," he thought, "It was something else - something indescribable but very intriguing." Josie opened his eyes and noticed that a little blue light was flickering and flashing in front of him. "Teddy? Is that you?" Josie whispered. There was no response, but the light grew larger and steadier and soon filled the entire room. Josie stepped out of his body and approached the light. Instantly he was flying in his dream body through a pure, white substance that looked like snow. "Where am I?" Josie said aloud.

A familiar voice answered, "We are in the *Land of the Warm Snows*, the home of the *Inner Master*." Josie looked to his left and saw Kim Starr and Melina flying next to him.

"I don't understand," Josie continued. "How did I get here?"

"The blue light you saw was an invitation from the *Inner Master*," Kim responded. "When you stepped into the light, you were transported here. Melina and I also received an invitation."

"Have you been here before?" Josie asked.

"Oh, yes, many times."

"Why is everything white?" Josie started. "At first, I thought it was snowing, but it feels too warm to be snow."

"The energy on the lower realms is both positive and negative - light and darkness, always seeking a perfect balance. The energy on the higher realms is pure positive – light without darkness. Our human minds are always trying to rationalize what they see, so we experience the pure positive energy as warm snow. The warmth comes from the unconditional love that the *Inner Master* has for all of God's creations."

Kim pointed towards a pinpoint of light in the distance and steered them in that direction. The light increased as they neared it, and when they reached its origin, Josie was surprised to see that it was emanating from a large mirror. The travelers touched down softly, and Kim explained, "This is the *Mirror of Truth*. When you look in the mirror, you will gain an understanding of your physical life in relation to your spiritual life."

"My spiritual life?" Josie remarked. "I don't understand."

"You may think of yourself as a physical being living a physical life, but you are actually a spiritual being living a physical life. The purpose of each physical life is to serve as a building block in a series of blocks to contribute to your overall spiritual growth and life. A physical life has a distinct beginning, middle, and end, but a spiritual life does not. It is eternal. Unfortunately, many live as if the physical life is all that matters. The tendency is to completely forget about building one's spiritual life, which is the very reason for the physical life."

"Why would we forget something as important as that?"

"Remembering is the whole point of a physical life. As spiritual beings, we know who and what we really are. The challenge is to remember this while living a physical life filled with distractions, emotions, and Maya's powerful influence. In this respect, the *Physical* serves as a testing ground for soul. We work on remembering who and what we are, lifetime after lifetime, while facing every scenario in creation. These cycles of incarnation continue until we remember who and what we are regardless of the circumstances we may find ourselves in."

"So, the mirror will show me how well I am doing, like a report card?" Josie asked hesitantly.

"No, but the mirror will lead you to a realization about what is standing in the way of you remembering who and what you are."

Josie reluctantly stepped forward and peered into the mirror. He didn't see anything, not even his own reflection. "I don't understand," Josie cried out, "It's empty."

Josie stood in stunned silence as a realization began to form. His life used to be filled with incredible spiritual adventures and knowledge, and now he felt as if it had no real meaning or purpose.

"My life is so empty," Josie cried out to Kim. "How will I ever fill it again?"

"Begin with acts of kindness," Kim whispered gently.

Josie inwardly vowed to do this. Kim and Melina took flight once again, and Josie followed suit. They traveled in silence for quite some time as Josie reflected on his spiritual life, and then his thoughts drifted to the *Inner Master*. "What is the *Inner Master* like?" Josie asked aloud.

"The *Inner Master* is a fountain of love, knowledge, and guidance and is best known through experience rather than description."

Josie was enthralled with the *Land of the Warm Snows*. There were many adventures they could have had that fine night, but they saved them up for another time and another story. They soon arrived at the *Temple Within*, where they found the *Inner Master* waiting for them. Josie wasn't sure whether his dream body had a heart, but he was certain that if it did, it was beating at least a thousand times a minute.

The *Inner Master* wasn't at all what Josie had expected, even though Josie wasn't quite sure what he had expected. At first sight, Josie thought that the *Inner Master* was a man, but then he seemed to change into a woman. The color of the *Inner Master's* skin was initially very dark but then grew lighter as it went through the entire range of skin tones. Josie rubbed his eyes and whispered to Kim, "I think there's something wrong with my eyes because it looks like the *Inner Master* keeps changing."

"There isn't anything wrong with your eyes," Kim whispered back. "The *Inner Master* holds the consciousness of every spiritual Master in creation and is all things to all people."

The *Inner Master* gestured for Josie to come forth. Josie felt ashamed by what the mirror had revealed about him, so he hesitated to make eye contact with the *Inner Master*. Then he worried that this might be deemed disrespectful, so he lifted his face and looked directly into the *Inner Master's* eyes. The *Inner Master* gazed deeply into Josie's eyes in return. Josie saw his true self reflected in the *Inner Master's* eyes. He was an incredibly beautiful spiritual being composed entirely of light and sound. It was a sight like no other he had ever seen. Josie didn't learn until much later in life that he had just received the Darshan, a special blessing from the Master.

CHAPTER 8

THE QUEST

Josie wished he could recall more about his visit with the *Inner Master*. The only things he did vividly remember were an exhilarating feeling of joy, a sense that everything was exactly how it was meant to be, and a flood of true happiness coursing through his being. He wanted to be able to feel that way every moment.

School was back in session, and Josie was anxious to talk to Kim again. He searched for her during recess and found her talking to a group of her friends. Josie didn't want to interrupt, so he waited on a nearby bench, hoping that she would notice him. She didn't, but Melina responded to his thoughts and whispered something into Kim's ear. Kim looked over her shoulder and spotted Josie. She said goodbye to her friends and approached him. Josie was elated when she sat down next to him and asked how he was doing.

"I'm better, different than I was before visiting the *Inner Master*. I came away from our visit with the overwhelming realization that I am meant to live in a constant state of true happiness. I'm just not sure of how to go about that. I could really use some guidance."

"I understand," Kim answered. "I am so fortunate to have Melina as my spirit guide, as you were to have Teddy."

"What?" A surprised Josie said.

"Teddy was my spirit guide?"

"Of course," Kim continued. "He introduced you to realms beyond the *Physical*, helped you navigate through them, and protected you from the negative. He opened up your mind to sacred knowledge and expanded your heart's capacity to love and be loved. He also set up scenarios to test your knowledge. That is what a spirit guide does."

"But I didn't know that."

"Do you think it would have made a difference if you had?"

"Well, if I am honest, it probably wouldn't have. I was feeling so uncomfortable and angry and felt like Teddy was the problem. I thought I needed to get rid of him so I could feel good again."

Melina spoke up, and when she did, her luminescent wings spread wide and fluttered like a butterfly. "Teddy wasn't the problem. Your discomfort was due to you losing your spiritual ignorance and becoming enlightened again. You spent many lifetimes wrapped in the darkness of spiritual ignorance, like a caterpillar wrapped in a cocoon. The cocoon is only comfortable in the early stages of a caterpillar's growth. It later becomes quite constrictive and uncomfortable. If it didn't, the butterfly would never emerge. Spiritual growth can also be quite uncomfortable at times, especially right before a major transformation is about to take place."

"Can you tell me how to live in a constant state of true happiness?" Josie asked.

"If you want to accomplish this, you must first discover the source of true happiness."

"Can the *Dream Train* take me there?"

"No, Josie, discovering the source is something you will have to achieve on your own. But I will give you a clue. The source lies within everyone and everything in creation."

Josie thanked Melina for her wisdom and said that he had one more question.

"Are all spirit guides fairies?"

Melina smiled, fluttered her spectacular wings, and answered. "Spirit guides can manifest in many different ways – human, animal, fairy, or any other form that will put a spiritual traveler at ease."

The bell rang to signal the end of recess. Kim and Melina said their farewells and headed inside. Josie stayed on the bench for a few extra minutes and made a solemn vow that he would begin his quest for the source that very day, and so he did.

Melina's words rang out in his memory. "The source lies within everyone and everything in creation." Josie snuck up on every animal, bird, tree, blade of grass, insect, and even rocks and streams without warning - in hopes of catching them and their secret off guard. He searched every moment that he could, but he never saw it or felt it.

Mary called Josie after school to see if he wanted to meet with her at the stable, but he politely declined. He wanted to get off the phone to continue his search, but he didn't want to hurt her feelings, so he asked her how the puppies were doing. She told him that four puppies had been adopted, but she wasn't sure if the fifth one would ever be adopted. "He's very sweet and loving with the members of my family, but whenever someone comes who is interested in adopting a puppy, he backs into a corner and growls and barks until the person leaves. None of the other puppies were like that."

"I'll try to come over soon," Josie said, hoping to cheer Mary up. He then hung up and went back to his search.

The next day a very weary Josie was too tired to go outside for recess, choosing instead to lay his head down on the top of his desk and take a nap. He closed his eyes, happy to be free of his quest for a short while. He was just about to slip out of his body when he heard soft crying out in the hallway. It sounded so pitiful and sad. Josie got up and followed the sound. It led him to Sammy, a small boy who was new to the school. Josie's heart stirred with compassion, and he asked, "What's wrong?"

"My legs," Sammy responded. "Butch was making fun of my legs and knocked me over." Josie looked down and saw that Sammy's legs had heavy metal braces on them. He reached out to Sammy and helped him get up off the floor.

"I think your braces are cool," Josie said. "They look heavy. You must be very strong to walk around in them all day. I bet you could kick a football right out of the field if you tried." Sammy dried his tears on the sleeve of his sweater, sniffled a couple of times, and then looked up at Josie and smiled. A wave of true happiness flooded through Josie and spilled out all over Sammy. Sammy giggled, and Josie's heart felt full. The bell rang, and the two boys had to return to their classrooms. Josie patted Sammy on the back and said, "Let's be pals. We can eat our lunches together every day and play games at recess." Sammy nodded eagerly, a definite yes.

Later that day, Josie was deep in thought about what might have caused him to experience the burst of true happiness. He had felt compassion for Sammy and reached out in kindness. Then bam, it happened, true happiness, but it slowly faded away as the day went on.

He had to find the source so he could feel it whenever he wanted to. In the meantime, he decided that he would focus on being kind at every opportunity because even a short burst of true happiness felt better than none.

Josie's days became filled with acts of kindness and compassion. He brought his teacher a nice shiny apple, opened doors for people, took out the trash for his mother without being asked, and picked up a book for a fellow student after she dropped it. Josie smiled at everyone he saw, including Butch, who at first looked suspiciously at Josie, but later grew to like it.

Josie was spending so much time and energy being kind that he barely had time to search for the source. He wondered if he would ever find it but took comfort in the many little bursts of true happiness he received throughout the day while loving and serving others.

Josie started to miss his friend Mary and decided it was time to visit her at the stables. He didn't tell her he was coming, and she jumped up and down with glee when she saw him. She ran over and gave him a great big hug. Boom! Another burst of true happiness coursed through Josie. San Shrie was tied to a post. Josie approached him with caution for fear that San Shrie would get upset again. San Shrie glanced over at Josie and nickered for him to come near. Josie went closer and extended his hand towards San Shrie's soft nose, which was waiting for a loving caress.

"I guess he changed a lot over the summer," Mary said.

"So did I," Josie responded before laughing out loud.

Mary, San Shrie, and Josie spent the rest of the afternoon at the stable. Josie felt several waves of true happiness during their time together and felt fully recharged when Mary mentioned Bonji's puppy again. Josie wondered if he might be able to do something nice to help the unhappy puppy feel better. He suggested this to Mary, and she eagerly took him up on his offer.

Josie was amazed at how the puppy had grown. He also found it interesting that aside from its black color, the puppy didn't look anything like Bonji. The puppy sat in the corner of the room and repeatedly cocked his head from one side to the other as if he was trying to figure something out.

"Get ready," Mary warned. "This is the part where he usually starts growling, barking, and snapping."

The puppy jumped up and down instead and made all sorts of happy sounds before bounding over to Josie. The puppy was wearing a smart, red collar and had the cutest, chubbiest little belly, and its long, energetic tail was wagging non-stop. Its hair had grown a lot since Josie had last seen it, and a tuft on the top of its head stood straight up.

Josie bent down and picked up the puppy, who wiggled in his arms. The puppy's fur was silky and soft, unlike its mother's. It reminded Josie of the way George's feathers used to feel. Josie closed his eyes to fully take in the puppy's sweet smell, and at that moment, he realized that everything about the puppy felt like George. Josie's heart began racing, then skipped a beat. "Could it be?" he wondered. "Is it possible?" Josie could barely breathe as he whispered softly, "George. Is it you?"

The puppy threw back his head and let out not one, not two, but three delicious barks, which sounded almost like rooster crows. Josie looked into the puppy's soulful eyes and realized that his quest was over. He had found the source of true happiness. It was love.

Mary was astounded by the puppy's reaction to Josie.

"It looks like a match made in Heaven," Mary said.

Josie was reminded of the day he spent in Heaven when he told George that he loved him, and George said, "I love you too, and I always will."

"Yes," Josie agreed. "It is a match that was made in Heaven."

It was immediately apparent to them both that the puppy was meant to be with Josie.

Josie was so happy to be reunited with George, but then a wave of sadness swept over him when he realized he couldn't share the news with Teddy. Josie hadn't wanted to admit it before, but he missed Teddy terribly. He felt deeply ashamed that he had ever sent Teddy away and sincerely wished to be with him again. As Josie's sadness increased, a lone tear trickled out of the corner of his eye and ran down his cheek. A very happy and stylishly dressed Teddy appeared on Josie's shoulder and dabbed the tear away with his teensy, tiny handkerchief.

THE END OF BOOK ONE

Teddy & Josie

A Preview of Book Two

Melina's Mission

CHAPTER 1

THE HIGH COUNCIL

The *High Council of Twelve* silently entered the garden through a wooden archway covered in a cascade of brilliant white, night-blooming jasmine. They moved in single procession towards the *Circle of Trust*, where twelve ornate thrones defined the circle. The thrones were most unusual because they were not carved out of wood; they were formed by wood. They were trees, which had sprung up from the garden floor and shaped themselves into thrones of different shapes and sizes to accommodate the council member's physical differences. (Three of the members were fairies, three were gnomes, three were devas, and three were nature spirits.) Each throne was gnarled and twisted into a perfect work of art. Small flowering vines crept into every nook and cranny and gently kissed and caressed the precious wood. The throne seats were smooth and comfortable due to the many thousands of years of use, and the seatbacks rose so high into the air that it was impossible to judge just how tall they were. Insects and birds, who ran rampant over the other trees in the garden, kept a respectful distance from the thrones, choosing instead to sit quietly nearby and bathe in their essence.

The thrones formed a perfect circle around a large, amethyst-lined geode that emitted a beautiful, pale, lavender light. Its appearance was soothing, and its energy stunning. Its radiance deeply moved the members as they entered the circle, one at a time, and announced their presence:

"Wakia, Kingdom of Sky."

"Loma, Kingdom of Earth."

"Mayspeena, Kingdom of Air."

"Ceanna, Kingdom of Water."

"Kon, Kingdom of Fire."

"Densia, Kingdom of Mammals."

"Kika, Kingdom of Birds."

"Bubulah, Kingdom of Fish."

"Sisk, Kingdom of Reptiles."

"Whisp, Kingdom of Insects."

"Versia, Kingdom of the Unseen."

Josie, with his fairy guide Teddy sitting in his customary place on Josie's left shoulder, sat outside the circle along with many others who had been invited. The council only gathered during the winter and summer solstices, the autumn and spring equinoxes, and in times of grave emergency. So, those in attendance grew unsettled for two reasons:

It was not a solstice or equinox and Satia, Kingdom of Flora, was not present.

Everyone sat in silence and then bowed their heads in reverence. Next, they took a few deep, relaxing breaths and began to sing the sacred Hu. Josie always loved doing the Hu song both by himself and with Teddy. It left him feeling centered, peaceful, and happy. This time was no different in that regard, but it was hugely different in another way. The energy of the entire group singing together was so powerful that it left no doubt in one's mind that all things were truly possible.

At the conclusion of the Hu song, a most beautiful and soft-spoken fairy approached the council and was granted permission to speak. "I, Melina, daughter of Satia, Kingdom of Flora, requested this meeting. Some months ago, my mother shared with me that she was very concerned about an alarming decrease in the number of blue flowers. As you know, the energy from the blue flowers sustains all of the other flowers, so if they cease to exist, the other flowers will soon follow suit. So Satia decided to journey throughout the kingdom in search of answers. She was scheduled to return before the summer solstice and is now long overdue." Just then, Whisp, Kingdom of Insects, spoke up. "One hundred of my bravest and noblest bees went out in search of Satia, and I am distressed to say they have completely vanished without the slightest trace. I sense that something dreadful is happening." The remaining members nodded in agreement and began to speak up about disturbing events that were taking place in their kingdoms. The devas, midwives of nature, who assist in the birthing of new life, shared that they witnessed a reluctance of new life to enter the physical reality. The nature spirits, who help new life lock into the physical reality and maintain its form, expressed concern over the number of life forms who had left, never to return again. The gnomes, who usually patrolled gardens in darkness to check for and remedy any imbalances, reported that they were working in the daylight as well to keep up with the devastation they were encountering. The council members listened to concerns about the quality and scarcity of water, the planet's rapid warming, changes in weather patterns, an increase in the number of earthquakes and volcanic eruptions, and an overall state of disruption. These situations were not new to the planet but did not usually occur simultaneously and with such increased frequency.

Every kingdom was being affected in alarming ways, and the council members were left with heavy hearts and grave concerns. Versia, Kingdom of the Unseen, arose and spoke. "I propose that the kingdoms join forces to search for Satia and to discover what is undermining the balance of all life on the planet. I sense that something sinister is afoot."

Master Rose Ashley was born in Philadelphia, Pennsylvania, shortly after the end of World War II. She grew up as an only child watching cowboys on TV and dreaming of one day living on a ranch out west with a trusty dog and a beautiful horse. Her dream didn't look as if it would rapidly  unfold because her father traveled extensively with the Navy and her mother worked a full-time job in the city. So, she entertained herself by reading books, visiting with spirit friends, and galloping throughout the house on an imaginary steed.

Master Rose is presently a spiritual teacher and advisor who served as a professional psychic for 15 years before being initiated in 1986 as a Master of the Swanéte philosophy. Swanéte is an ancient spiritual philosophy based on a core belief that we are here to love and serve God by loving and serving all of God's creations. Her primary areas of exploration are metaphysical studies, parapsychology, quantum physics, and animal communication, rehabilitation, and training. Her signature workshop of over 35 years is *Inventing Your Life*, a pathway to spiritual success and true happiness.

Her two passions in life are helping people and helping animals, which led her to establish *The Swan Center for Intuitive Living* in 1987. The Swan Center is a spiritual, educational center for those seeking higher levels of personal awareness and is also a sanctuary for previously abused and neglected horses. Master Rose and her students rescue and rehabilitate horses then partner with them to offer spiritual and therapeutic programs for children and adults, including those who are mentally and physically challenged.

Master Rose loves introducing people from every walk of life to the therapeutic and spiritual value of a loving relationship with animals. She presently lives out west in the Santa Clarita Valley in California with two trusty dogs, an entire herd of beautiful horses and one miniature donkey. She spends her time teaching spiritual classes, writing, working with animals, and doing as many arts and crafts as she can possibly squeeze into her day.

For more information, please feel free to visit us at:

www.SwanCenter.org

Or contact us via email at:

Inquiry@SwanCenter.org

www.ingramcontent.com/pod-product-compliance
Lightning Source LLC
Chambersburg PA
CBHW051810050726
47598CB00006B/2505